Next steps in supporting people with autistic spectrum conditions

Series Editor: Lesley Barcham

Mandatory unit and Common Induction Standards titles

Communicating effectively with people with a learning disability
ISBN 978 0 85725 510 5

Personal development for learning disability workers ISBN 978 0 85725 609 6

Equality and inclusion for learning disability workers ISBN 978 0 85725 514 3

Duty of care for learning disability workers ISBN 978 0 85725 613 3

Principles of safeguarding and protection for learning disability workers
ISBN 978 0 85725 506 8

Person centred approaches when supporting people with a learning disability
ISBN 978 0 85725 625 6

The role of the learning disability worker ISBN 978 0 85725 637 9

Handling information for learning disability workers ISBN 978 0 85725 633 1

Titles supporting a unit from the level 2 health and social care qualifications

An introduction to supporting people with autistic spectrum conditions
ISBN 978 0 85725 710 7

An introduction to supporting people with a learning disability
ISBN 978 0 85725 709 3

Titles supporting a unit from the level 3 health and social care qualifications

Promoting positive behaviour when supporting people with a learning
disability and people with autism ISBN 978 0 85725 713 0

Next steps in supporting people with autistic spectrum conditions
ISBN 978 0 85275 705 5

Next steps in supporting people with autistic spectrum conditions

Sue Hatton and John Simpson

Supporting a unit from the level 3 health and
social care qualifications

Los Angeles | London | New Delhi
Singapore | Washington DC

all about people

all about people

Learning Matters
An imprint of SAGE Publications Ltd
1 Oliver's Yard
55 City Road
London EC1Y 1SP

SAGE Publications Inc.
2455 Teller Road
Thousand Oaks, California 91320

SAGE Publications India Pvt Ltd
B 1/I 1 Mohan Cooperative Industrial Area
Mathura Road
New Delhi 110 044

SAGE Publications Asia-Pacific Pte Ltd
3 Church Street
#10–04 Samsung Hub
Singapore 049483

Editor: Luke Block
Production controller: Chris Marke
Project management: Deer Park Productions
Marketing manager: Tamara Navaratnam
Cover design: Pentacor
Typeset by: Pantek Media, Maidstone, Kent
Printed by: Ashford Colour Press Ltd, Gosport, Hants

BILD
Campion House
Green Street
Kidderminster
Worcestershire
DY10 1JL
© 2012 BILD

First published in 2012 jointly by Learning Matters Ltd
and the British Institute of Learning Disabilities.

British Library Cataloguing in Publication Data

A catalogue record for this book is available from the
British Library

ISBN 978 0 85725 705 5 (pbk)

ISBN 978 0 85725 850 2

Contents

This book covers:

- The Level 3 health and social care unit LD 310 – Understand how to support individuals with autistic spectrum conditions

Acknowledgements

Photographs from www.crocstockimages.com, www.shutterstock.com, www.careimages.com and Photosymbols.

Our thanks to Sue Hatton, John Simpson and his family, Edward and Elizabeth Attfield and family, Tom Boughton, Choices Housing and Autism Plus for their help.

About the authors and the people who contributed to this book

Sue Hatton

Sue Hatton is a teacher by training and worked in schools and then two further education colleges. In the last 16 years Sue has worked for an autism specific charity as their learning and development manager and as an autism adviser for a national health and social care company. She now works for Studio 3 Training on their ATLASS (Autism Training Low Arousal and Specialist Support) programme. Throughout her career Sue has sought to establish working relationships with people she has taught or supported in order to involve them in staff learning and development. John and Sue met when John was attending a discussion group for adults with Asperger syndrome and Sue was a facilitator for the group. It did not take long for Sue to realise that John had the potential to be a good speaker and advocate for people with autism and they soon began to work together quite regularly and learn from each other. This is a journey that they have continued over the last eight years.

Sue has a Master's degree with a special study in autistic spectrum conditions. She has co-authored two other BILD books, one with a woman with Asperger syndrome, *Conversations in Autism – from insight to good practice*, and one co-written with Tom Boughton, *An Introduction to Supporting People with Autistic Spectrum Conditions*, which is in this series.

Several people have made a contribution to this book and Sue and John are grateful for their honesty and willingness to share their story to help others gain a better understanding of autistic spectrum conditions.

John Simpson

John is a very capable young man who was expected to be a high achiever while in school. At 16 years of age John was admitted to a child and adolescent mental health ward suffering with severe mental ill health. He remained there for six months and this is where he first received his diagnosis. However, it was not until much later and as part of a discussion group for people with Asperger syndrome that John came to understand what his diagnosis meant. Then his journey began, not only to better mental health, but also to learning how to keep well in an autism friendly way. John gives regular presentations to a wide range of parents and professionals as someone living with an autistic spectrum condition and his particular contribution when speaking is the link between mental health issues and autism. John also works part time as a support worker in a care home for adults with autism and severe learning disabilities.

Carole and David Simpson

Both John's parents kindly agreed to talk about their experience of raising John, the struggles as a family when John had his mental health problems and the experience of getting a diagnosis for John with no real guidance as to what that meant. They went through some very dark times, but today are very proud of all John has achieved and the way he can hold an audience when he gives a presentation about his life with an autistic spectrum condition. John has a brother who kindly shared some of his experiences as well.

Elizabeth Attfield and Linda Woodcock

These two friends and colleagues who both have adult sons with autism remain guiding lights and good reminders of the importance of listening to the whole family in order to be able to provide effective and appropriate good support for individuals.

Alex Calver and Tom Boughton

These two young men with autism worked on the book, *An Introduction to Supporting People with Autistic Spectrum Conditions* for this series, and they have continued to make a contribution to this book, sharing more of their life experiences of living with autism.

Naomi Owereh

Naomi's editing skills and knowledge of autism and many of the individuals referred to in this book have been invaluable; she has made an important contribution, for which Sue and John are very grateful.

Introduction

Who is this book for?

Next Steps in Supporting People with Autistic Spectrum Conditions is for you if you:

- want comprehensive information on how to provide good support to a person with autism;

- are a worker or volunteer in an organisation such as a college, leisure centre, community or health centre and you occasionally provide services to people with an autistic spectrum condition;

- work in health or social care with people with autism or people with a learning disability who also have autism and you want a better understanding of people's needs so that you can provide good support;

- are a manager in a service supporting people with autistic spectrum conditions or people with a learning disability and autism and you have training or supervisory responsibility for the development of your staff;

- are a direct payment or personal budget user and are planning learning opportunities for your personal assistant.

This book builds on the learning from *An Introduction to Supporting People with Autistic Spectrum Conditions* by Sue Hatton and Tom Boughton.

Links to qualifications

This book gives you all the information you need to complete the level 3 unit, *Understand how to support individuals with autistic spectrum conditions*, from the level 3 diploma in health and social care, as well as the level 3 learning disability certificate and award. You may use the learning from this book to:

- work towards a full qualification, e.g. the level 3 diploma in health and social care;

- achieve accreditation for a single unit on autism awareness.

Although anyone studying for the qualifications will find the book useful, it is particularly helpful for people who provide services to or who support a person with autism. The messages and stories used in this book are from people with an autistic spectrum condition, family carers and people working with them.

Links to assessment

If you are studying for this unit and want to gain accreditation towards a qualification, first of all you will need to make sure that you are registered with an awarding organisation who offers the qualification. Then you will need to provide a portfolio of evidence for assessment. The person responsible for training within your organisation will advise you about registering with an awarding organisation and give you information about the type of evidence you will need to provide for assessment. You can also get additional information from BILD. For more information about qualifications and assessment, go to the BILD website: www.bild.org.uk/qualifications

How this book is organised

Generally each chapter covers one learning outcome from the qualification unit *Understand how to support individuals with autistic spectrum conditions*. The learning outcomes covered are clearly highlighted at the beginning of each chapter. Each chapter starts with a story from a person with autism or a family carer or worker. This introduces the topic and is intended to help you think about the topic from their point of view. Each chapter contains:

Thinking points – to help you reflect on your practice;

Stories – examples of good support from people with learning disabilities and family carers;

Activities – for you to use to help you to think about your work with people with learning disabilities;

Key points – a summary of the main messages in that chapter;

References and where to go for more information – useful references to help further study.

At the end of the book there is:

A glossary – explaining specialist language in plain English;

An index – to help you look up a particular topic easily.

Study skills

Studying for a qualification can be very rewarding. However, it can be daunting if you have not studied for a long time, or are wondering how to fit your studies into an already busy life. The BILD website contains lots of advice to help you to study successfully, including information about effective reading, taking notes, organising your time, using the internet for research. For further information, go to www.bild.org.uk/qualifications

Chapter 1

Understanding the main characteristics of autistic spectrum conditions

One evening I went to visit a friend whose 10-year-old son, Danny, has an autistic spectrum condition. I have been to the house many times before and Danny knows me well. As I knocked on the door I could hear that my friend was on the phone. She called to her son to open the door. Danny did this and stared at me. It was going dark and I thought maybe he could not see me properly so I said, 'Danny, it's me, Sue.' Danny replied, 'I know who you are', and shut the door!

His mum finished her call, opened the door and asked me in, apologising for what appeared to be Danny's rather rude behaviour.

We sat together in the kitchen talking and having a cup of tea. Suddenly Danny came rushing in talking about his cars and repeating a description of a new one he wanted. His mum tried to get him to stop talking as once again he was appearing very rude, but as she tried to reason with him he got more and more animated about the car and would not stop talking. Then my friend behaved in what appeared to me to be a rather strange way with her child. She lifted her hand up and put it close to Danny's face and said, 'Danny. Stop. Recorder practice. Now.' With her other hand she had picked up a recorder and some music which she gave to Danny. Danny stopped talking, took the items and went into the other room and played his recorder.

Sue Hatton

Introduction

I often find the best way to help people understand the nature of autistic spectrum conditions is to tell a story. The above story about Danny sounds rather strange and will encourage the reader to ask questions, such as, 'Why on earth would he behave like that?' or, 'Did he not understand what was said?' These questions can lead to a full exploration of the impact autism has upon an individual, their family and others who support them.

Autistic spectrum conditions are complex. To have a good understanding of an individual you will have to analyse their behaviour carefully and build up layers of understanding over time. If you do have a good understanding of autistic spectrum conditions, then you will know that the simplest of things can solve problems for the person and for those who are working with them. Spending time seeking to learn about and understand an individual's autism is invaluable and can make a huge difference to their lives.

Learning outcomes

This chapter will help you to:

- analyse the diagnostic features of autistic spectrum conditions;
- explain the meaning of the term 'spectrum' in relation to autism and the key conditions on the autistic spectrum;
- describe language issues for people with autistic spectrum conditions;
- understand the sensory difficulties and differences for people with autistic spectrum conditions;
- explain the other conditions associated with autism;
- explain why it is important to recognise that each person on the autistic spectrum has their own abilities, needs, strengths, gifts and interests.

This chapter covers:

Level 3 LD 301 – Understand how to support individuals with autistic spectrum conditions: Learning Outcome 1

A word about language

Language is developing all the time, and the words we use to describe a particular impairment or disability change as a result of listening to people with personal experience, as a result of changing values and attitudes in society and as a result of new research. The terminology used to describe the autistic spectrum has changed over time. The terminology used in this book to describe the autistic spectrum is autistic spectrum condition (ASC); this is one of several common usages at the time of writing. The term autistic spectrum disorder is still used sometimes in more clinical or research settings. The term autism is often used, and is still widely accepted, as an umbrella term for the spectrum, for example by organisations such as the National Autistic Society. Autistic spectrum conditions has been chosen for this book as it is a more neutral and less medical term than autistic spectrum disorder. When you are working with a person with autism listen to the words they and their family use to describe their condition and then if you are comfortable take your lead from them.

Diagnostic features of autistic spectrum conditions

In the short account about Danny at the beginning of this chapter you can begin to see some of the diagnostic features of autistic spectrum conditions. Danny is an able boy who attends a mainstream school but he has difficulties in the three key areas that are still known as the 'triad of impairments', as identified by Dr Lorna Wing in 1981. Danny talks well, especially when he is talking about his toy car collection. However, he has difficulty understanding language and can take things very literally. He was asked to open the door but because his mum was not explicit in telling him to also ask me into the house, he did not KNOW to do this. This also shows social communication difficulties, as most children aged 10 would do the socially polite thing, if they knew the person at the door, and would have invited me in. They certainly would not have shut the door in my face in the way Danny did, or have spoken to me in what appeared to be such a rude manner.

The appearance of rudeness continued as he interrupted my conversation with his mum. This may not be that unusual in itself, but what did seem strange was then to go on and on and on about the same car, saying the same things over and over again, as if he was working himself up into quite a frenzy. What I did not know was that Danny was confused by my arrival. His mum had not told him I was coming – which was a big mistake on her part, she told me later.

This change in his evening routine with things happening in an unpredictable way caused him to feel anxious. When anxious, Danny retreats into his 'special interest' and the more anxious he gets, the faster he talks about his cars. Fortunately, Danny's mum knew how to get things back on to an even keel for Danny. She spoke clearly, using as few words as possible. She gave visual clues to what Danny needed to do – the hand held up near his face, the recorder and music in front of him. This very familiar, predictable activity, brought calm. Danny was then able to do his recorder practice for 15 minutes. After 12 minutes, my friend explained she would now need to go through his bedtime routine which would take about 20 minutes and then we could talk some more.

What appeared to be the behaviour of a rude child was something else. Danny has an autistic spectrum condition and with the right help and support he can and does cope in a mainstream school. It is hard work for Danny, his teachers and his family and takes considerable understanding, time and effort. However, all of this effort is worth it, and Danny lives a happy and rich life in the 'neurotypical' world.

The diagnostic criteria for autistic spectrum conditions are currently being reviewed and refined, a process which will be completed in 2013. For the psychologists, psychiatrists and others involved in diagnosing people with autism this means that the source of diagnostic information, the *Diagnostic and Statistical Manual of Mental Disorder*, fourth edition, which is produced by the American Psychiatric Association, will be changing in 2013. This is because there is a regular review process for the way diagnosis is understood, and the year 2013 is the appointed time to review autism. The most usual route for a person to get a diagnosis is via their GP and a referral to a specialist in the field. However, referrals can also come from a teacher, parent and from the individual themselves.

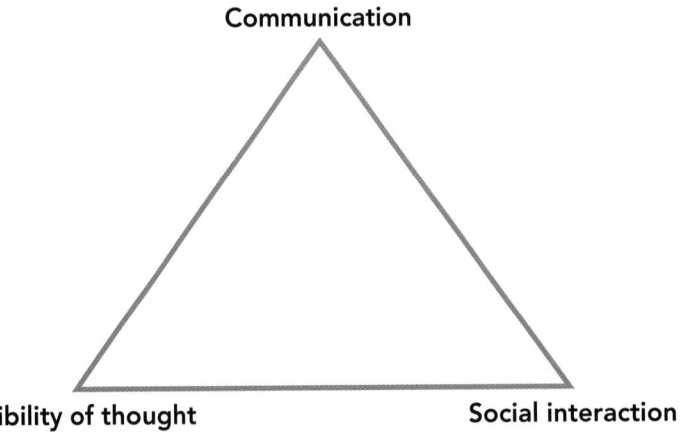

The triad of impairments.

Dr Lorna Wing, in her book, *The Autism Spectrum* (1981) has had a powerful influence on our understanding of the nature of autistic spectrum conditions. She introduced the idea of the 'triad of impairments' in 1981and she set out three main areas of difficulty that are experienced by people with autism. These are:

- problems with social interactions and relationships;

- difficulties with language and communication;

- problems with the imagination that results in inflexibility in ways of thinking.

It is these three areas that have traditionally been referred to as the 'triad of impairments'. In 2013, two areas of the triad are likely to merge as they are so interrelated, that is communication and social interaction. In addition, it is now increasingly understood that people with autism experience their senses differently to others and that this too needs to be considered when making a diagnosis.

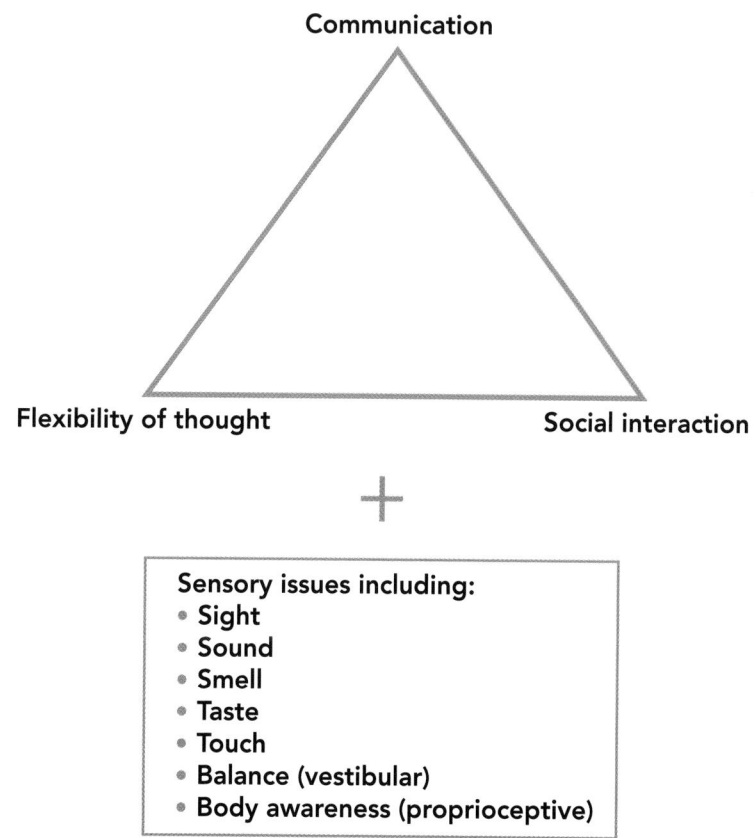

The triad of impairments and sensory issues.

Language and communication difficulties

Danny's story makes it clear that communication is not just about someone's ability to speak or not. It is much more about their ability to actually communicate their needs through a two-way process of social communication that is so hard to understand when you have autism.

As with the other book on autism in this series, *An Introduction to Supporting People with Autistic Spectrum Conditions*, I have been working with someone with an autistic spectrum condition and his family to ensure that the information you are reading is really grounded in the life experience of having autism. John Simpson and his mum and dad have made a big contribution to this book. John is a good talker and when you first meet him you would perhaps not notice that he had any particular difficulties. He attended mainstream school until his anxiety and stress levels led to mental ill health, which was when he finally received his diagnosis of an autistic spectrum condition.

David, John's dad, says:
Even when John was at nursery school he was good at talking to our friends, but he did not make friends of his own very easily. We felt this was rather charming to begin with, but that did not last.

John says:
I find it difficult to know how to start a conversation unless it is about football or buses and I can't work out when people have had enough of listening to me talk.

Those of you who work with individuals who are non verbal or have minimal language may think that John and his family will not be able to help you understand the people you work with. You are wrong. Getting to know some more able people with autism, and listening to how they see the world, gives us an incredible insight into *everyone* with autistic spectrum conditions. It is about understanding the broad facets of autism better and then looking at how it impacts upon each individual. The best way to do this is to listen to those who live with autism and can explain a little about their lives.

John works part time as a support worker in a residential care home with people who have autism and learning disabilities. He has some very valuable insights into their communication issues.

> *John explains:*
>
> Zack is always anxious when it comes to the weekly shopping day. He struggles to get into the kitchen as the food is being unpacked and there have been a number of incidents at this time. Staff worry about Zack in the kitchen as he has no awareness of danger, and because he does not speak, staff tend to think his understanding is equally limited, but it isn't. The oven chips we have are one of Zack's favourite foods and the only reason he wants to get in to the kitchen is to check that they have brought back oven chips, of the right brand and that there are plenty. I persuaded staff to let me take Zack into the kitchen with the shopping bags. We emptied them out onto the table and he put all the bags of frozen oven chips together. He looked at them, touched them and smiled, and then left the kitchen happy. This is now a weekly routine and there have been no more incidents. Zack is not able to explain about what makes him anxious other than with behaviour that people often misinterpret. Like me, he has a communication problem. I like to look at bus timetables when I am anxious as I find them predictable and calming. Zack just needs to know each week that there are lots of bags of the right kind of oven chips.

John has told me that in many ways he feels more connected to those individuals he supports who have autism and severe learning disabilities than he does to his work colleagues. He knows the way people with autism think, because he has autism too. When we have the opportunity, we need to really listen to people like John if we are to improve our own understanding and working practices.

Social interaction and relationships difficulties

The second part of the triad focuses on the social interaction difficulties that people with autistic spectrum conditions experience. This is where we see difficulties with friendships and in understanding how relationships actually work. A very able woman with autism, Temple Grandin, the author of many books and a regular speaker at conferences, said at an event in 2009 that she continues to find the way people relate to each other a 'complete mystery, … it is as if there is some kind of secret code that people have and I can't work it out'.

I believe that this can be a particularly hard part of having autism in a family because the relationship you have as a parent with your son or daughter or as a sibling is so different. It is hard also to see a member of your family struggle with making friends and this often leads to the isolated life that people with autism can appear to have. However, we do need to take care about making easy assumptions. John does like to see people and he will refer to some individuals as friends, but these are relationships that have to happen in an ordered and predictable way for John. He is able to explain how important time alone in his room with his bus timetables is, and how utterly exhausting he finds social interaction.

When working with individuals who are not able to explain their feelings we need to take care that there is the right amount of social interaction. We need to learn how to get alongside people, to value their special interests and share them if possible. However, we also need to allow them 'down time' where they are not being confronted with what is exhausting – namely the social expectations of others. People with autism need their own space, but not too much of it. In order to maintain good mental health and well being we need to help people with autism to learn the value of human interaction. It is vital that this interaction is done in an autism friendly way.

Do we ensure that we inform the people with more severe learning disabilities whom we support about what is happening, and when, in terms of social expectations? We could improve the way we communicate information by using photos. We could tell them that they will be going on the bus to the supermarket using a photo sequence. We might then wonder why an incident occurs or the person seems anxious, as we explained the activity using autism friendly methods. However, if we examine our communication more deeply, we would realise that we did not make clear that other people living in the home would be joining in the trip, and it is this missing information that has made the individual anxious.

Problems with ways of thinking or impairment of the imagination

The third area of the triad is referred to as the 'impairment of the imagination'. It is very much about the need that people with autism have for predictability and the difficulties they have with coping with change. John says that for him, every day is a 'quest for predictability'. His levels of anxiety rise rapidly when unexpected events happen. John finds fire alarms stressful and so do many other people with autism. As people supporting those with autistic spectrum conditions, we need to think of ways of making the unpredictable less scary and this can be a huge challenge. One service I know has been very creative with a man with autism who is terrified of the fire alarm and unable to move when it goes off. On the wall of his bedroom is a laminated pair of footprints that were made by drawing around his feet. The set routine is that when the fire alarm goes off, he collects his footprints from the wall, goes downstairs and out into the back garden to the assembly point. On the ground there is a concrete slab with another pair of footprints that he drew around with paint. He places his laminated footprints on the footprints on the concrete slab and then stands on them. Giving him this simple and yet very visual predictable routine has enabled him to cope with the fire alarm and fire practice and evacuate the building like everyone else. Being autism friendly requires imagination and thinking outside of the 'neurotypical' boundaries.

The spectrum of autism

Autism is spoken of as a 'spectrum' condition. However, it is not just about some people being very able and some people having a severe learning disability. This is too simple an explanation. Thinking like this leads to people seeing John, who is verbally competent, as far more able than he actually is in certain situations. Such a view of the spectrum also leads to people making the assumption that Zack has very little ability in any area because he is non verbal. The reality is more complicated and we need to take time to consider this. John can help us with an understanding of what is known as the 'uneven cognitive profile of autism'.

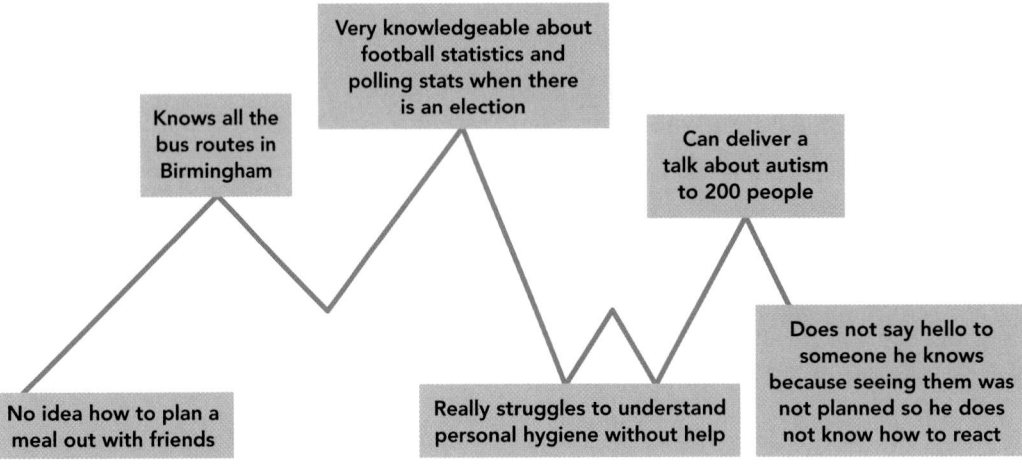

John's uneven profile.

John says:

John says:

Many people with autism have an uneven cognitive profile. This means that they may be massively skilled in one or several small parts of their life, but may have massive skills gaps in other areas. Typically this can lead to immense frustration both with and for the individual. In my case it meant that at school I was capable of learning, understanding and excelling when asked to comprehend complex mathematical equations or use difficult historical concepts as evidence in a piece of writing. But understanding why no one liked me or working out how to competently use scissors completely eluded me.

The spectrum is about the severity of the autism and the kind of impact it has in different areas of life alongside the level of learning ability or disability. I know an individual with a diagnosis of severe learning disability and autism who is non verbal, but if you empty the pieces of a one hundred piece jigsaw on to the table they are able to complete it very quickly and face down – taking no notice of the picture on the box.

We need to learn not to make assumptions about the individuals we work with and actually recognise this uneven profile. As we find out about them we need to be looking for the things they find easy or excel at, as well as the things they struggle with and then work with the reality of this uneven profile. At times this can be frustrating, but at other times you can be amazed at what individuals can achieve.

John's mum Carole says:

I have to support John to enable him to do his part time job at the residential care home. This means making sure he has everything he needs for the bus journey there: the right change for the bus, keys, his phone and his headphones for when he is travelling. John is not able to sort these things for himself even though he is able to talk at a conference to 200 people about his autism – something that would terrify me. I do get frustrated but I have learnt that things I find simple, for John are an incredible challenge and vice versa.

Understanding the main characteristics of autistic spectrum conditions is not enough on its own as a basis for learning how to support people with autism effectively. You also need to be aware of the spectrum of autism, and of the range that can be found within it.

In thinking about a spectrum we need to consider the severity of the person's autism and also the nature of their learning ability or disability. A learning disability includes the presence of a significantly reduced ability to understand new or complex information and to learn new skills together with a reduced ability to cope independently. A person's learning disability would start before adulthood, and it would have a lasting effect on their development.

The labels we attach to certain parts of the spectrum are a guide and do not indicate clear-cut boundaries between one condition and another. One form of autism tends to merge into another, and sometimes it can be unclear where on the spectrum an individual stands. This does not matter greatly, provided enough is understood about the person's needs in order to ensure that they receive all the necessary and appropriate support.

Learning disabilities can also be seen as a spectrum. Many people with autism, particularly those receiving support, will also have a learning disability, and that learning disability may be anything from profound to mild in nature. These individuals will also have difficulty in the areas described previously and will need 'autism friendly' support. The book, *An Introduction to Supporting People with a Learning Disability* by Elaine Hardie and Liz Tilly, in this series, provides a lot of useful information on the nature and characteristics of learning disability.

We will now look at the main characteristics of some key conditions on the autistic spectrum:

- Classic or Kanner's autism;
- Pervasive developmental disorder not otherwise specified (PDD-NOS);
- High-functioning autism;
- Asperger syndrome.

Do not be put off by the fact that these labels appear to come from a medical model of autism, which focuses on diagnosing and treating an illness or condition. They are widely used and there is no reason why a label of autism cannot be a basis for organising holistic care and support based on a social model of disability. The social model of disability says that a person is disabled by the barriers in society. For many people with autism, the barriers they experience are caused by people's attitude and prejudice towards them and their autism.

Classic autism

This is also referred to as **Kanner's autism** in recognition of the observations on the condition published by Leo Kanner in 1943.

- All three areas of the triad of impairments will be present as well as sensory processing difficulties.
- There will be difficulty with social interactions, including indifference to other people, one-sided interactions, and an inability to understand the reactions of others.
- Problems will occur in social communication, such as not understanding tone of voice or facial expressions, or finding it hard to communicate by word or gesture.
- There will be limited imagination or rigidity in activities or pursuits, often combined with repetitive or obsessive approaches.

Pervasive developmental disorder not otherwise specified (PDD-NOS)

As mentioned at the start of this chapter, autism is itself a pervasive developmental disability. A pervasive disability is one that affects many areas of development. However, PDD-NOS is used where someone has severe and pervasive impairments in all three parts of the triad of impairments, but does not meet the criteria for a specific disorder.

Wendy Lawson, who has an autistic spectrum condition, points out that this may be no more than saying we do not know what is wrong. She expresses concern that a diagnosis of this kind may be confusing and unhelpful.

High-functioning autism

The usual, and useful, meaning of this description is that the person has an autism spectrum condition, but does not have a learning disability. Be aware that this term is sometimes used as if it had the same meaning as Asperger syndrome. It is essential to remember the uneven cognitive profile even when someone is very able or high functioning, as the individual may well surprise you by being very able and yet not grasping things that seem very obvious or simple.

> *John says:*
> I understand about the need to wash underwear and socks every day but I really don't understand how you know when to wash your trousers or a jumper.

Asperger syndrome

Asperger syndrome is a condition described by Hans Asperger in 1944; the year after Kanner published his observations. When later it was realised that people with Kanner's autism and Asperger syndrome have much in common, the term 'autism spectrum disorders' was coined. Now the term 'autism spectrum condition' is also in use. If autism is seen as a continuum, Asperger syndrome is often described as close to, or merging into, high-functioning autism. Some people think they are the same thing and others feel it is important to make a distinction.

The areas which classic autism and Asperger syndrome have in common tend to be mapped to the main characteristics of autism:

- difficulties in social relationships;

- problems in communicating;

- poor ability with flexible thinking, not understanding what goes on in other people's heads and a need for predictability;

- sensory processing difficulties and differences.

There are also areas in which they differ. For a diagnosis of Asperger syndrome, the person will have:

- normal development of speech and language, though still a problem with two way communication;

- an absence of a learning disability (but still an uneven cognitive profile as referred to by John earlier);

- an average or higher level of intelligence.

The conditions we have looked at are labels. These may be useful in ensuring that the right services and support are given to people with autism, but should never be allowed to detract from their individuality as human beings. The main characteristics of the autism spectrum should be used to enable you to appreciate the diversity of the people you support, and the range of their needs.

Language issues and autistic spectrum conditions

As communication is one of the major difficulties for people with autistic spectrum conditions, we need to think carefully about the language we use to communicate and equally we need to think about the way in which people with autism may use language. I worked with a young man once who only spoke using phrases from his favourite DVDs, which were about Thomas the Tank Engine. There were lots of people he called the Fat Controller, after a character from the DVDs. We came to realise this had nothing to do with their weight, but that this label was connected to their status and how important he felt they were. It was usually the most senior member of staff on duty who was called the Fat Controller for the day. How he knew which members of staff were senior staff I have no idea, but he did, which is a great example of the uneven cognitive profile. He would also sometimes repeat over and over again, 'Careful on the tracks there, careful on the tracks there'. We soon realised that this also really meant something. He said it when he was bothered about what was happening to him or if he saw something dangerous, for example a man at the top of a ladder was once greeted by the phrase many times over. This young man was clearly anxious about the man being up a ladder and the only way he was able to express his anxiety was through the Thomas the Tank Engine language he was comfortable with. For him this had meaning. We need to listen carefully to what people say and not think that their language has no meaning just because it does not seem to make sense to us. This point is well made by Phoebe Caldwell in her work on the use of intensive interaction. She speaks of 'learning the language' when working with people with autism and severe learning disabilities.

It is possible that you are supporting a person who has little or no verbal language, but they communicate well with noises, and the way they behave makes certain messages very clear. If you know the individual well then you will be able to recognise happy, sad or anxious sounds. This is where really getting to know someone and THEIR autism is so important. For many people who don't use much speech, or any at all, then a communication passport can be helpful. A communication passport is a person centred small leaflet or book to help others understand the different ways an individual communicates their feelings and needs.

Activity

Find out if a person you know with autism has a communication passport or any other communication information. If they do, carefully read this and consider if it is up to date or if it needs reviewing to ensure it is relevant for that person's current communication needs. If you don't know anyone with a communication passport or profile do some research about them and discuss your findings with colleagues.

When communicating with a person with autism, it is important not to make any assumptions about the way they express themselves. In addition, we need to consider our own ways of communication. This includes the complexity of language that we use, our body language, and our tone of voice. It is important for staff to have a good level of self knowledge to be aware of the impact we have when using language and any non verbal ways of communicating. It is important to keep our language clear and precise and to try and ensure that we say what we mean and mean what we say.

When communicating with a person with autism, don't make any assumptions about the way they express themselves.

Sensory differences and difficulties

This is a big area of concern for many people with autistic spectrum conditions and though it has not formed part of the diagnostic criteria in the past, this is likely to change in the future. So many able people with autism talk of the huge difficulties they have with sensory issues that debilitate them and have an adverse impact on their lives.

John says:

My sensory issues are perhaps not as severe as other individuals on the spectrum. However, there are certain noises that have caused me real issues in the past. Typically, most of these occurred at school, and this is no coincidence. School was probably no noisier than many of the other places I visited as a child. However, school was the place where the anxieties I endured as a child were by far the highest. Anxiety massively increases the impact of any negative sensory experience of any individual with autism. I am able to stand on a station platform and watch, listen and feel as a 125mph train passes no more than a couple of yards away from me without the slightest degree of anxiety, and yet the school bell being rung caused me to be virtually frozen with fear.

The essential differences between the two are that at the station I am relaxed and that I can see the train coming. Surprise and heightened anxiety massively exacerbate the effects of any sensory experience, and I can honestly say my experiences at school could have been very different if someone had warned me just before the bell was going to ring.

Wendy Lawson, who has written a number of books about her life with autism, puts her sensory issues in a very vivid way in her book, Life Behind Glass (1998):

For some people, comfort can be found in a bottle of wine, good music, a good book, a good friend and a long walk, but for me soft materials, rocking to and fro, sucking the roof of my mouth, bright colours, routine and reassurance are able to calm and comfort me. Robbed of these things I am like a wild lion or a bat without its radar, and I can crash miserably!

If these are the reactions and feelings of some very able people with an autistic spectrum condition who can tell us and explain to us about their sensory issues, what must it be like for those who are non verbal or less able to explain?

Angie

Angie has autism and learning disabilities. She lives in a residential home with five other individuals who also have autism. There are times in the day when she gets very agitated and will bang doors, scream and bite herself. Staff have been trying hard to provide a good structure to the day and to be aware of Angie's needs, but these outbursts clearly distress her and her staff. In order to try and understand why these outbursts occur, the staff team began to complete ABC charts (antecedents, behaviour and consequences charts). This meant noting what the behaviour was that indicated Angie's distress, what was happening just before it started (the antecedent to the behaviour), and also the consequences of her behaving in this way. A clear pattern was soon revealed. It showed that Angie's outbursts followed a staff changeover, when the house was busy and noisier than usual, or when visitors came to the house and there was another increase in noise levels, or if one of the other residents was distressed and once again the noise levels in the house went up. This was very helpful information. Although it was not possible to completely stop these things happening in the house, it was feasible to try and prepare Angie and ensure she was in a place far away from the sudden increase in noise. In addition, Angie was offered headphones to wear and she could soon cope with the issue herself by carrying the headphones around and putting them on when she felt anxious about the noise. This led to a decrease in her anxiety and her challenging behaviour.

You can find out more about using records of incidents of challenging behaviour to understand the person and their needs in the book *Promoting Positive Behaviour* by Sharon Paley in this series.

Good support for people with autism can so often happen when we use simple ideas and very accessible tools. However, first must come the understanding. With Angie it was important to understand how truly painful she found the noise. This was so painful that she needed to make lots of noise of her own to block out the noise that scared and distressed her.

Issues around noise are very common for people with autism. We need to be aware of all seven senses and take into account the way each individual with an autistic spectrum condition experiences each of them. Building up a sensory profile for each person will really help you to understand how their autism has an impact and therefore how you can support them best.

Our senses are:

- hearing;
- vision;
- touch;
- taste;
- smell;
- balance – sometimes referred to as our vestibular sense;
- spatial awareness – sometimes known as our proprioceptive sense.

I want to look at the impact of the senses though two short stories about people who understood their own sensory needs. This helps to explain how we need to understand this aspect in relation to the people we support.

I was once presenting at a conference and a young man put his hand up to ask a question. He then asked me if it was OK if he looked at the floor whilst I was speaking because he really wanted to hear my answer. I asked if he could explain to people why he needed to do this – which he did.

> I really want to hear what Sue says but with her big earrings and bright top and coloured scarf I cannot possibly hear what she says if I am looking at her.

He then looked at the floor and asked his question. I answered him and he sat back down again. I felt we had all learnt a little more about the sensory issues around vision in autism.

Once I was carrying out a training session with a colleague who has autism and I touched her on the shoulder as we were sharing the talk together. I thought she would have seen my hand coming to her shoulder, but when I touched her she screamed and jumped backwards saying something had touched her. I explained it had been me and apologised and we were able to carry on. Later on we discussed what had happened and she explained it from her point of view:

> I know where my hand is and I can choose to put my hand on my neck. I know where my neck is and so I know it is my hand touching my neck. But if someone else touches me it does not make sense and I can't figure out what is happening and that is scary.

This may seem very strange to us but at least my colleague was able to explain to me how she felt and I now try hard to give her advanced warning if I am going to touch her. Interestingly, this same individual really wants to be touched when she is crossing a road. She finds it impossible to know what the cars are doing and how fast they are going so unless there is a crossing with lights, she likes to hold your arm very tightly, shut her eyes and run across with you.

Food is an issue for many people with autistic spectrum conditions and often relates to their inability to tolerate particular textures, smells and tastes. Several able people talk about being scared of food that is a colour they are not able to tolerate or is of a particular texture. Creating strict and specific food patterns can be a way of bringing order out of confusion and ensuring that they have control over what can be frightening. Of course, there are those for whom the food and eating issues become quite serious and this can be a tremendous source of anxiety for families and those supporting them. If you can, try to appear relaxed and calm and only ever introduce something new in very small amounts and when the rest of the eating experience is as predictable as possible.

Paula

As part of a circle of support for Paula we were trying to encourage her to eat different foods. This was something she wanted to do and we tried to make it predictable by choosing places to eat so Paula knew what kinds of food to expect. There were three different venues we were using for this work. I recall one occasion when Paula was well prepared to have five bean chilli for her meal at one of the chosen venues. We tended to go for an early lunch when the places were not crowded. On this particular occasion when we got inside and sat down Paula suddenly said, 'It is going to have to be jacket potato and cheese for me today.' I was both baffled and disappointed as the introduction of new foods had been going well. Once we were sitting down with our meals I asked Paula what the problem was. 'In this pub we usually sit at that table over there, and if I have to sit at a different table I can't possibly try new food – it is just too much.'

Paula's words teach us that trying to ensure as much 'sameness' as possible for an individual with autism is key when we are planning to introduce something new.

When I deliver training on understanding autism and talk about the senses, most people say they are not aware of any issues about the sense of smell. I certainly have worked with many people for whom their sense of smell does not seem to be that different to my own. However, occasionally I have met someone for whom their sense of smell is a real issue and often it has been in how they seem to identify people and know who we are. Many people with autism tell us that they find it difficult to remember faces, but for some it would seem they really do use their sense of smell to know who people are and this can cause some problems.

Spatial awareness or the proprioceptive sense is the one that most people find surprising. Think about how stress and anxiety can mean that your spatial awareness gets worse and means that you are more likely to crash into people and objects and appear very clumsy. This can help you to identify when spatial awareness becomes a problem for the people you work with. This is not true for all people with autism and some have very good spatial awareness and balance. However, many really struggle with knowing where their body is in relation to their environment and this again can be quite scary. People with problems with their sense of balance can also have proprioception difficulties.

Abdul

Abdul lives on his own with support coming in each day. He understands his autistic spectrum condition reasonably well and this includes knowledge about his own sensory difficulties. In the past Abdul has got into trouble for shouting at people in the street for crashing into him, particularly people who have been pushing a buggy with a child in it. As you can imagine, this has not been received very well and Abdul has been in trouble a few times with the police. The self awareness work he has done has made a huge difference to his behaviour, and one of the decisions he took with this new understanding was to go to the supermarket at 10pm at night rather than during the day when it was busy. The supermarket aisles had previously been a place of real conflict. Abdul says he hardly ever meets anyone pushing a buggy or a trolley at this time of night. He can shop and remain calm and so is much less anxious. He has also started to stand still when a buggy is coming towards him in the street in order for the person pushing it to navigate round him. Once again this has decreased his anxiety.

I have chosen to share these stories to encourage you to think where you can make the connections for those people you support who have sensory differences and difficulties due to the impact of their autistic spectrum conditions. There is much still to learn in this area but a good sensory assessment by an occupational therapist who knows about both autism and sensory integration can be really helpful with suggestions for making life easier for individuals.

Thinking point

If you have ever broken your arm or leg you may recall how it felt when the plaster cast came off after six weeks. For a short while, it is as if your arm or leg will not do what you tell it to do and it feels very strange. This is your proprioceptive sense adjusting and it can take a while for the brain to be able to transmit messages to your limb accurately. For some people with autism, this is a difficulty they have every day. Try to remember this next time someone with autism bumps into you.

Other associated conditions

It is quite common for people with an autism spectrum condition to have an additional condition. The National Autistic Society tells us at least 70% of people who have autism also have an additional condition. For example, you may know a person with:

- autism and epilepsy;
- autism and bowel problems;
- autism and a restricted or very specific diet;
- an autistic spectrum condition and a mental health problem;
- autism and an additional genetic condition like Fragile X syndrome or Down's syndrome.

Ensuring individuals get really good support when their autism is combined with other conditions presents an even greater challenge. It is vital to really get to know the individual and think deeply about the complexity of their needs.

The one condition that we perhaps need to focus on and understand is something the majority of people with autism struggle with and that is anxiety. Their deep desire for predictability in a world that is so uncertain produces stress and anxiety. As staff, we need to work hard to maintain our awareness of this and also to do all we can to reduce the anxiety levels.

When John gives talks about his autism he often asks people how they feel when they have an important job interview and how the anxiety they speak of affects them. Answers are varied but often include things like:

- checking the time frequently;
- unable to eat much;

- having a dry mouth;

- a sense of panic.

John suggests that people who can identify with the feelings and actions due to anxiety over a job interview need to be aware that this is the everyday experience for people with autism. This may lead to them checking things, rituals like touching the floor so many times before they go through a door or switching lights off and on. It may lead to rocking, teeth grinding and numerous other behaviours that are a result of heightened anxiety. Very often, people can be helped by something quite simple, especially if it is predictable. This can include:

- the same greeting routine when a staff member comes on shift;

- a set pattern for getting up that is supported and followed by everyone;

- a piece of music that is known and liked;

- early morning exercise like a long walk before breakfast – but a known walk that is predictable.

If we can work at finding out how to reduce the anxiety that people experience then we will be supporting individuals towards a much better life.

Thinking point

What happens to you when you feel anxious? Consider how you would feel if this happened every day.

Activity

Try to think of one thing you could do regularly to help reduce the anxiety of someone you work with. Do it, and if it works talk to your colleagues and see if all of you can work together to reduce the levels of anxiety for those you support.

Recognising each person on the autistic spectrum has their own abilities, needs, strengths, gifts and interests

Autism is a developmental disability. This means that it arises in infancy or early childhood, and results in the delayed development of abilities such as language and play with others. Autism affects an individual for their entire life, especially their communication, social interaction, ways of thinking and behaving, and their senses.

It is important to remember that each person with autism is an individual, having their own unique personality, family and community culture. In order to be truly person centred, we need to be aware of every aspect of who they are and learn to value what is important to them, no matter how strange or unusual it may be to us. For example, one person with an autistic spectrum condition that I know is extremely interested in windows and he loves to talk about the different kinds of windows you can find in buildings. Being willing both to listen and to share in this interest is a key way of giving this person both respect and acceptance. This is equally true for someone with more severe learning disabilities and autism who may enjoy sifting sand. Not only is it important to allow this to happen and encourage what they enjoy to really show a sense of value, it is also worth sharing the experience. This may sound a little strange and we should not just leave someone sifting sand all day, but there is something about valuing what they value if we are to be person centred.

If you are to work in a person centred way with a person with autism there are three points on which you should be clear. These will help you in understanding each person's unique gifts and talents, dreams and ambitions alongside their support needs.

1. Autism is a spectrum of conditions. It has different effects on different people. Although all people with autism share certain characteristics they are individuals and must be treated as such. Working in a person centred way is important. To do this for someone with autism we have to understand *their* autism.

2. The model of the triad of impairments is still widely used to understand autism and it is extremely important to know the impact of each area within the triad on the person you support. But do not underestimate the impact of sensory issues for every person with autistic spectrum conditions.

3. In your experience when supporting a person with autism, taking a positive and person centred approach is paramount. Whilst autism leads to some difficulties and challenges, equally it is vital to recognise an individual's gifts and abilities and once again to value them and use them if you are to be truly person centred. If someone is very tidy and likes to make sure everything is in its place, involve them in the housework. If someone is good with bus numbers and bus routes, give them responsibility for teaching new staff the best bus routes to different places. People with autism have much to offer and you need to let the person you work with know that you appreciate their gifts and skills.

References and where to go for more information

References

American Psychiatric Association (1994) *Diagnostic Statistical Manual (DSM IV), fourth edition.* Arlington, VA: American Psychiatric Association

Beardon, L and Worton, D (2011) *Aspies on Mental Health: Speaking for ourselves.* London: Jessica Kingsley

Bogdashina, O (2003) *Sensory Perceptual Issues in Autism and Asperger Syndrome.* London: Jessica Kingsley

Caldwell, P (2007) *From Isolation to Intimacy – Making friends without words.* London: Jessica Kingsley

Grandin, T (2000) *Sensory Challenges and Answers.* Arlington, TX: Future Horizons Inc.

Grandin, T (2005) *Thinking in Pictures and other Reports from My Life with Autism.* New York: Doubleday

Hardie, E and Tilly, L (2012) *An Introduction to Supporting People with a Learning Disability.* London: Sage/Learning Matters/BILD

Hatton, S and Boughton, T (2011) *An Introduction to Supporting People with Autistic Spectrum Conditions.* Exeter: Learning Matters/BILD

Jordan, R (2001) *Autism with Severe Learning Disabilities.* London: Souvenir Press

Lawson, W (1998) *Life Behind Glass.* London: Jessica Kingsley

Mukhopadhyay, T R (2008) *How Can I Talk if My Lips Don't Move?* New York: Arcade Publishing

Paley, S (2012) *Promoting Positive Behaviour when Supporting People with a Learning Disability and People with Autism.* London: Sage/Learning Matters/BILD

Wing, L (2003) *The Autistic Spectrum.* London: Robinson Publishers

Websites

National Autistic Society www.autism.org.uk

OASIS – for information and support for families, individuals and professionals www.aspergersyndrome.org

Phoebe Caldwell – for more information about her DVDs and books www.phoebecaldwell.co.uk

Chapter 2

Understanding how an autistic spectrum condition can impact on the life of an individual and those around them

When John became ill, which eventually led to his diagnosis of Asperger syndrome, we blamed ourselves. Why had we not picked this up properly before? We tried to put a brave face on things but we felt awful and we felt we had failed as parents. We also felt isolated and depressed and seemed unable to comfort each other. It was a frightening time.

John's mum and dad

I did not know there could be such a thing as 'too good a baby'. He was so content and never cried; he never seemed to want to be picked up. At first I thought I was lucky, but then I began to realise there was a problem and this was not normal. It wasn't until he was four that we finally got a diagnosis of severe autism.

Elizabeth – mum to Edward

Introduction

Both the families quoted above were on a journey of discovery with their child, like all parents, but they found themselves going in a different direction than they had anticipated. Elizabeth often says it was like getting on a plane to go to one destination and discovering you are somewhere else. The language is different and you have come with the wrong things in your suitcase but in time you learn about this new place and find a new way forward. There is, of course, a considerable struggle and many parents talk of feeling very alone, as the experience of having a child who is different can be very isolating. But Elizabeth, and John's mum and dad, will also talk of their pride in their sons.

Support for families is crucial and the ability to share your experience with other people who really do understand because they have gone on a very similar journey can be extremely helpful. Parent support groups may not suit everyone but there is no doubt that for many families they are a life line.

Learning outcomes

This chapter will help you to:

- describe the impact of autism on the life of the person with the condition and also the impact on their parents or carers, siblings and others who are close to them;

- explain how the person's gender, ethnicity, social, cultural and religious environments might impact on their experiences;

- explain how stereotypical views, discrimination and a lack of understanding of autism can make things worse for the person with autism, their family and others who are close to them;

- describe ways of helping a person with autism and their parents or carers, siblings or partner to understand their autistic spectrum conditions better.

This chapter covers:

Level 3 LD 301 – Understand how to support individuals with autistic spectrum conditions: Learning Outcome 2

The impact of autistic spectrum conditions

We will begin with a few quotes from parents of people with autistic spectrum conditions to give a sense of the impact it can have on families.

Margaret, mum to Jake, says:
My beautiful, healthy, bouncing baby turned into a tornado of destruction. By the time he was three, there wasn't a playgroup or nursery that would have him. I felt very alone.

> *David, dad to John, says:*
> He would talk to us all as if he was on the same level – it felt a bit spooky… he related to us as equals and peers and I found this strange.

Having a child with autism is really a 'slow dawning' for most families and, if it is the first child in the family, then it can take longer for parents to realise that there is something different about their son or daughter. The impact and effect of the autism is different for each person. The family experience can vary, but when a child fails to progress with their peers in certain key areas then families often begin to ask questions.

Elizabeth talks of her concern and at times embarrassment when other children at playgroup interacted with each other and with the toys provided, whilst her son Edward only wanted to spend time spinning the wheels of his pushchair.

John's mum recalls that she was aware of John's poor hand eye coordination from early on and the concern of his teachers because he was unable to hop. However, as he was being put in for higher-level SATS exams she just put it to the back of her mind.

What became true for both Elizabeth and Carole, John's mum, was the reduction of their social life, even though they had friends with children of a similar age, because the differences with their child became so marked in a social setting.

> *Carole, John's mum, says:*
> His brother joined in with our friends' children but John did not, would not and could not. It became more obvious especially as he kept wanting to spend time with the adults and this meant we could not speak to our friends in the way we wanted to because John was always there.

John and his brother shared a room when they were young and they did play board games together. For Sophie, Edward's sister, it was hard having a brother who was very obviously different. This meant that she did not want to bring friends home until she was older and more able to understand, and expect others to also understand, about her brother's autism.

Many parents talk about having to try and make sure that they give time to their child or children without autism, rather than doing things as a family altogether. This puts logistical strains upon families and it is not surprising that the figures for relationship difficulties and breakdowns are very high amongst families where a child has a disability and even higher if that disability is an autistic spectrum condition.

In her book, *Living with Autistic Spectrum Disorders* (2007), Elizabeth Attfield refers to the strain on families as a whole and on the siblings without autism: 'The siblings' own behaviour may deteriorate as an attention seeking strategy, causing parents further stress, or they may worry about parents not coping and the family splitting up, especially if there is a lot of family disharmony.'

The sense of loss and feeling of 'I must be to blame' can become acute and very painful. Families work through this in different ways and one of the things professionals can do is to be prepared to listen to their story. You will then have some level of understanding of their feelings, although it is never completely possible to stand in their shoes. Giving our time to listen is so important.

You can find out more about working in partnership with family carers in the book, *Partnership Working with Family Carers of People with a Learning Disability and People with Autism*, by Alison Cowen and Jamie Hanson, which is part of this series.

All too often, parents of individuals with autism get a reputation for being pushy or awkward. I have heard staff say many times things like, 'Well, it must have been hard being Sam's mum when he was at home but there is no need for her to go on at us all the time. We are caring for Sam now and we do know him.' If you are tempted to think like that, stop and try and find out more about what it was like for the family of the person you are supporting when he or she was growing up. Invite mum in to share her journey and stories with the staff team. The experience of being the parent or sibling of a person with autism does not cease when the person becomes 18, or when they leave home. So often, their son or daughter is not leaving home to become independent and make their own life. Instead, it is often a struggle to find the right place for their child and the right support. Even if a successful new home is found with good support, mum and dad often remain the main constant in the life of the person, carrying the worry and concern of who will go to visit when they are no longer able to. All parents want the best for their children, but most will experience the time when you have to let them go so that they can make their own decisions and lead their own lives. If your son or daughter has autism, the experience of 'letting go' is very different and never fully happens, no matter how good the supported living service might be or the staff at the residential care home.

The impact and effect of autism is different for each person and for each family.

Thinking point

It is useful for us to try and put ourselves in the shoes of the parents or carers of those we work with and support. However, we also need to remember that this is not really possible and the closest we can get is to actually listen to the mum or dad. Have you ever done that? Have you done it often enough? Never forget the years of caring that parents and other family members have done and the worry and anxiety they will have about their son or daughter's future.

Activity

Why don't you ask one of the parents you work with to share their journey with you? Take care with how you approach this, but perhaps tell them you are learning more about autism and that you have learnt that understanding the views and feelings of parents is very important. If this is successful, you could ask them to talk to a group of staff.

Gender, ethnicity and the person's social, cultural and religious environment

Until recently it was thought that autistic spectrum conditions affect far more boys than girls. Ratios of four to one and even as high as ten to one have been cited. But more recently there has been a growing body of work, by Gould and Ashton Smith (2011), which documents evidence of girls being undiagnosed or misdiagnosed. We need to think carefully about gender and not make assumptions too quickly. Like boys, girls on the autism spectrum will have special interests. These special interests may be more socially acceptable and less isolating than some of the interests boys may have. Girls' interests can often focus on animals or toy collections or certain pop stars. This may also be true for boys, but more often for them it can be something that surprises you and makes them stand out more from their peers. Examples of some of those more unusual interests I have come across recently are:

- electricity pylons;
- the dog on an insurance advert on TV;
- traffic lights;
- battles fought on English soil where the King died on the battlefield;
- windows.

Currently there are far more males than females receiving a diagnosis. However, do not make the mistake of thinking this is purely a male condition. Autism may present differently in women and girls, but the challenges they face because of their autism can be just as debilitating and they may need as much support. Sometimes they may require even more support as girls can be more aware of their differences and feel more isolated because of it.

> *Nicola, who has Asperger syndrome, says:*
> I had no friends at school apart from a girl who could not walk properly and had a calliper on her leg. Because we were both the odd ones out I always got put with her and she was sort of my friend but I never saw her out of school and we did not really talk to each other.

Tony Attwood, in his *Complete Guide to Asperger Syndrome* (2008), says that girls are better at watching their peers and imitating them, whereas boys fail to realise that this might be useful to them. Boys speak about being completely baffled by friendships and how they work. Some years ago, Shamus, a 16 year old with Asperger syndrome asked if he could talk to me. We arranged a time and a date and he wanted to talk whilst we walked a dog round a field, as this meant there was no need to sit opposite or look at each other. As we set off he asked me a question.

> *Shamus said:*
>
> Right Sue – you know about autism and Asperger's, so you know about me. I need you to tell me how to get a friend. What do I have to do? I need you to explain it to me as we walk the dog round the field so that I can get a friend tomorrow when I go back to school.

Girls and boys are different and this is true of those who have an autistic spectrum condition. The key areas of difficulty are of course present in both genders, but just may present in different ways. The examples above from Nicola and Shamus are about the struggle to grasp how relationships work and what social interaction is all about. This is one of the impacts of having an autistic spectrum condition.

Temple Grandin often says that life for people with autism was easier in the 1950s, as she feels that, socially, things were more rule-governed and therefore easier to grasp and follow for someone with autism. Today, so often we may say one thing to an individual with an autistic spectrum condition about what is appropriate behaviour. Then, when they watch TV, they see lots of people behaving in what has been described to them as an inappropriate way and this can be confusing. The social structures and ways of behaving in Western society are often very subtle now and we learn to be intuitive about our behaviour rather than following set rules. This is hard for people with autism and can make them much more vulnerable.

There are some cultures where those with a disability are likely to be hidden and kept from view. For some people, having a disabled child can be seen as shameful, or even as a punishment for something the family have done wrong. It may seem strange to some of us, but disability is still a very real fear in some parts of the world and in some cultures. We need to understand this if we are to offer good support to people with autism and their families who may come from different cultures.

Hand in Hand is a community for disabled children and young people in rural Ghana. I have visited Hand in Hand several times to help improve the understanding of autism for those who work there and care for the children. Almost all of the children and young people who live there have been abandoned because of the cultural beliefs about children with disabilities in their community. These beliefs do not only exist in rural cultures. In both the developing world, and in our own society, negative attitudes towards children and adults with a disability are often still prevalent. These attitudes need to be sensitively challenged wherever they occur, but they also need to be listened to if we are to support individuals and families to respond positively to people with autism. We must help people to see the inherent value of a human life, no matter who the person is, or in what way they are different from the majority in society.

I find that many people with autism enjoy spending time in religious buildings or with practitioners of different religions. This includes cathedrals and large churches as well as mosques and temples, as there are many of them and there is lots of uniformity. Such spacious buildings, echoing and laid out according to religious rules, can be calming for some. I recently spent a pleasant time in a cathedral with a person with autism who notably calmed once inside the building. He sat looking and watching and enjoying the sensory experience of the space, occasionally clapping and enjoying the echo of his own clap.

Being person centred means providing support that respects the person's culture and religious beliefs.

I also know those who find comfort and security in the rituals offered by following a certain religious path. This can include the ritual of meditation, eating at set times and learning the original language of the scripture associated with a particular religion.

> *Peter, who has Asperger syndrome, says:*
> I enjoy being a Buddhist. I love the rules and regulations about how you should interact with the monks at the temple. It all helps me to feel calm and purposeful. There is much to learn and this is a powerful special interest for me, now I am calm and my life has not always been like this.

Activity

Try and find out about attitudes to disability in different cultures either through research or by asking a colleague who is from another part of the world. Find out about the dominant attitudes towards disabled people and the type of education and support that is provided.

The impact of stereotypical views, discrimination and a lack of understanding about autism

Many years ago I went to work in a residential special school for pupils with autism. Before the first pupils arrived we had an open day for the community to come and visit and look around. One of the close neighbours came in with his wife and I was assigned to show them the building and to talk about the school. The husband of the couple was rather surly as we walked round and did not say very much. Then he turned to me and said, 'This autism, aren't they just bad and naughty boys who need a good hiding?' His wife was clearly embarrassed and tried to usher him towards the tea and coffee whilst apologising to me, but it was not the first time, or indeed the last, that I have heard that kind of comment.

Autism is a hidden disability in so many ways. If you sat in a pub talking to John about football you would probably just go home thinking he was a football fanatic, which he is. However, if you then saw him the next day at the bus stop and he ignored you, your opinion might change to thinking he is a rude and ignorant young man who has been brought up with no manners. You would, of course, be very wrong. Here is John's story about seeing me when he was not expecting to.

> *John says:*
> I was going to the office where Sue worked at the time but I was not going to see Sue. I was thinking about the person I was going to see and what I would say when I got there. I was preparing myself in the way I usually do. I rang the doorbell and was a bit shocked when Sue answered the door. I had not prepared to meet Sue and was going to see Vicky so I walked in as she had opened the door, said nothing, and went upstairs for my appointment. When Sue and I next met, at a time I was expecting to see her, she asked me why I had been so rude. I was a bit surprised as I did not think I had been rude. Sue explained that what I had done was walk past her without even saying hello, and this was rude. I explained to Sue that I was not prepared to see her and had not planned what I would say. She found this odd but as we talked I realised that I always plan what I will say and have set things to start conversations off with people, otherwise it can be a bit worrying not knowing what will happen or who will say what. With Sue I often ask her about her dog as he was in the paper once for getting stuck in a drain and the fire brigade had to rescue him. This is always a good way of starting the conversation. With other people I talk about different things related to them that I have prepared beforehand. So if I see people when I am not expecting to, I find it difficult because I am not prepared. Now I realise that I can appear rude. Now I am going to have to have some emergency conversations ready so that I can cope with these unexpected meetings.

Maybe John's story can help us to understand why, on a home visit to an individual I taught at college, he just kept saying 'no college' and pushed me out of the door. So often people with autism can be considered rude, but this is because much of our social behaviour is intuitive and it is that intuition that people with autism don't have. This can be very hard to explain to people who have little or no knowledge of autism and can be the root cause of many negative attitudes.

There are many other stereotypical views that people have developed about autism, most of which are unhelpful, because they are not true. The movie *Rain Man* did more than probably any other film to raise the profile of autism, but it also led to the idea that everyone with autism is brilliant at something like numbers, as was the case of the character played by Dustin Hoffman in the film. There are a number of people who have an autistic spectrum condition, who do have unbelievable talents or what is sometimes known as 'savant skills'. For example, Daniel Tamet, who learnt to speak Icelandic in three weeks, or the astonishing to-scale drawings and paintings of the artist Stephen Wiltshire. However, these individuals are exceptional and though we know that all people on the spectrum have an uneven or spiky profile of abilities, only very few have 'savant skills'.

It can be very upsetting for parents if they are asked, 'Do you know yet? What is he going to be brilliant at? Must be amazing to have a son who is so clever at one thing!' This can be especially upsetting if they are struggling to come to terms with their son or daughter's challenging behaviours and under-achievement in so many areas.

There is so much to be done to challenge negative attitudes about autism. Here are some of the many false assumptions you might enounter:

- People with autism don't give any eye contact

Some do and some do not! Some people with autism stare. Many are confused by eye contact and that is the key factor because it is part of how we socialise and communicate – both of which are areas of difficulty for people with autism.

- People with autism prefer to be alone

Some do and some do not! Some people with autism like to be alone so they can focus on their special interests. Others are scared of being on their own as they don't know what to do and have great difficulty structuring their time alone. It is the nature and value of relationships that are confusing for people with autism. There is a real need for good teaching and good support about how to develop friendships and how to value spending time with others. These things bring purpose and meaning to life, even if you have an autistic spectrum condition.

- People with autism are obsessed with trains

Some people with autism do love trains, but not all of them! Trains can be a special interest and the person may derive real pleasure from their many different aspects. There is, however, a key difference between having a special interest in something that can be intense and all absorbing, and being obsessed with something. Usually when people have an obsession the object or the activity does not bring them much pleasure. The object or activity ends up controlling them in a negative way. However, for people with autism their special interests are the source of great pleasure.

The reality is that it is important to understand the nature of the autism for the individual you are supporting. There are, of course, many links and similarities between all people with autistic spectrum conditions, but individuals have their own personalities and so there are also key differences. What is vital is that you get to know each person and <u>their</u> autism.

> *John says:*
> I work in a care home for people with autism. Although I feel a real affinity to the people and can understand so much about why they behave in the way they do, that can annoy and irritate other staff. I am also very aware of how different each person is. Autism affects people differently and those of us who work with people must recognise this if we are to be any good at our job.

Thinking point

Is there an assumption that you made in the past that now you know is not correct about people with autism? What made you change your mind?

Activity

Discuss the stereotypical views you hear people talk about in relation to autism with one of your colleagues. See how many different views the two of you can come up with. Talk about what you can do to help challenge some of these false ideas about autism and how you can promote positive and more accurate ideas about people with autism.

Help in finding a better understanding of autistic spectrum conditions

The National Autistic Society, or a regional autism charity, is often the first place families will turn to for help and support. Many find it helpful to listen to a story that is similar to their own from another family. It can be very helpful and comforting. Many will scour the internet for information or pay a visit to the library.

John's mum Carole says:

Books! I have found books on autism really helpful. I also value John's willingness to talk about his autistic spectrum condition. We can talk together and understand each other better. We still get frustrated with each other at times. Also professionals that we have been involved with, like those at Autism West Midlands and the staff who work for Aspire (an employment service); people there have really helped John and helped me.

John's dad David says:

Talking to our friends and my boss at work, this really helped to begin with.

Elizabeth says:

Meeting other parents who are in the same situation – there is nothing like it! Then you discover you are not alone. So often when I talk to parents now, that is what they say, that they don't feel so alone anymore. Having a child with autism can be very isolating and to find people who really understand, who are living with similar experiences to you, can be such a relief.

Other parents say that the workshops and training they have been able to access have been of great help, particularly if those delivering the training are parents themselves – this can make such a difference. Hearing people with autism speaking can make you realise what some people can achieve. This has been of particular value to John himself and has given him the impetus to share his own personal experiences. John will say that he gets pleasure from knowing he has been helpful to people. His real motivator for helping with training, however, is the fee he gets which helps to pay for the various things that are important to him such as:

- a season ticket to watch a well-known football team;
- Sky TV in his bedroom so he can watch all of the sport he likes.

John has something extremely valuable to say in relation to staff or family members who are trying to help someone understand the nature of their own autistic spectrum condition.

> *John says:*
> Sue has helped me to realise that the more I talk about my autism, the better I understand it and how it affects me. It is as if speaking about it and telling the same stories over and over again really enables me to understand myself better. With an improved understanding I then seem to be able to move on and tackle new challenges. I am not able to do this in my head, the kind of internal self-reflection that Sue tells me 'neurotypical' people do. In order to think about myself and to learn from that thinking, I actually need to talk and tell my story. This is how I learn. So not only do I earn the money I want and need, I am also developing much better self awareness and I am told this improves my talks.

Self-awareness is essential as the foundation for the development of social skills for people with autism. 'The building blocks to social competency come naturally to most neurotypically developing children, but when a child has autism they need to be taught' (Hatton and Tector 2010).

This could be as basic as an ability to recognise yourself in the mirror, and to know if you have dirt on your face or a blob of cream on your nose. It is also about knowing you are male or female, and recognising yourself in a photo from many years ago. There is so much to be done in this important area, for all people with autism.

One of the most useful tools in addressing self-awareness is a life storybook. Collecting photos of an individual as a baby, child and young person, and then photos of activities the individual likes to do and some of their family members – all of these help to build a sense of self. Photographs provide a concrete, visual aid that can help many with autism cope with concepts such as 'self' and 'time'. The digital camera is one of our most beneficial tools for the support of self-awareness. For those who are able to talk about themselves, being given the opportunities to speak about their autism will be of benefit. My experience with John and with others I work with is that each time they deliver a talk about themselves and their autism they add a little bit, because they have become more self aware. This does not seem to be possible without the repetition and going over of the same story. Going over their story again and again allows new ideas to form and new understanding to take place in their own minds.

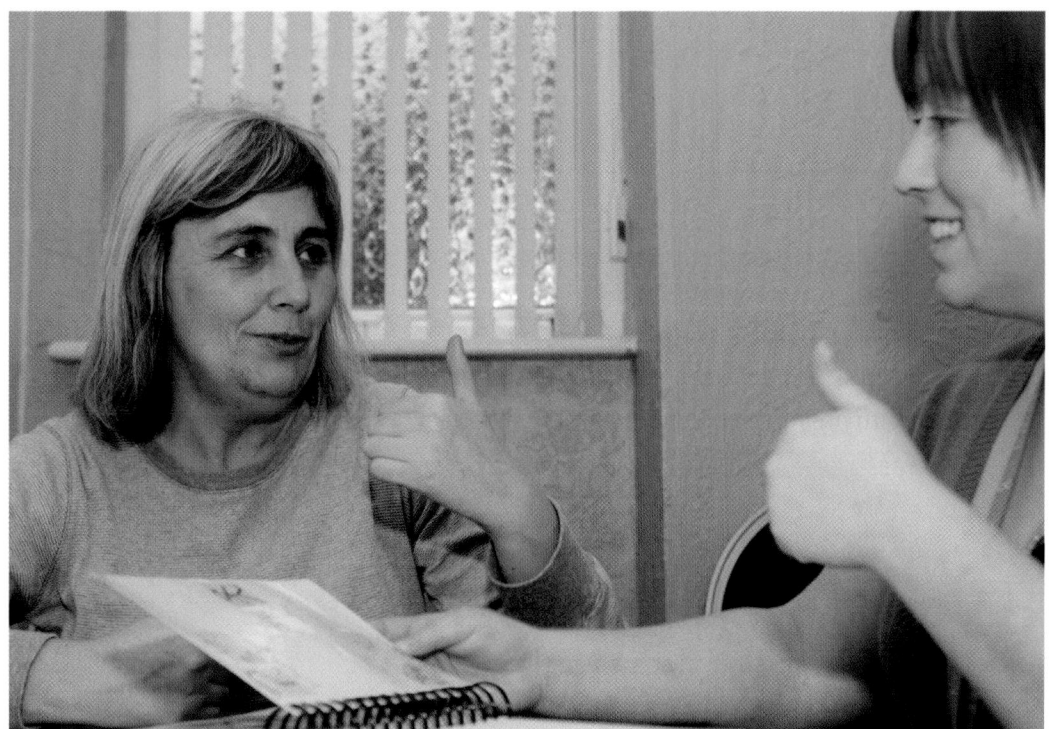
A life storybook can be a useful tool in developing self awareness.

For others, the journey of self knowledge may be slower and quite limited, but still vital. Edward, Elizabeth's son, enjoys looking at photos of family holidays and playing the game of having the wrong name given to his sister and making noises until mum gets it right. This is all part of knowing who he is and seeing his place in the world. A valued place as a member of his family and the community he now lives in.

The longer term future is hard for the families of those with autism and the individuals themselves. I asked John's mum about her concerns for the future.

John's mum says:
We live more in the immediate, like John does, it is a way of coping.

This is an important concept to grasp. Living in the immediate is the reality for most people with autism. We know they find it difficult to wait and that is partly because they do not understand why there is a need to wait, but we need to find ways of supporting the ability of families to look into and plan for the longer term future.

Key points from this chapter

- Never make assumptions about people with autism. They are all different and the impact of their autism in their life will be different.

- There are good support networks for families in many parts of the country and families need support and encouragement to seek them out.

- Listen to family members and give them an opportunity to tell you their story.

References and where to go for more information

References

Attfield, E and Morgan, H (2007) *Living with Autistic Spectrum Disorders.* London: Paul Chapman Publishing

Attwood, T (2008) *Complete Guide to Asperger Syndrome.* London: Jessica Kingsley

Attwood, T et al. (2006) *Asperger's Syndrome and Girls.* Houston, TX: Future Horizons Inc.

Cowen, A and Hanson, J (2012) *Partnership Working with Family Carers of People with a Learning Disability and People with Autism.* Kidderminster: BILD

Gould, J and Ashton-Smith, J (2011) Missed diagnosis or misdiagnosis? Girls and women on the autism spectrum. *Good Autism Practice Journal,* Volume 12, Issue 1, pp. 34–41

Hatton, S and Tector, A (2010) Sexuality and relationship education for young people with autistic spectrum disorder. *British Journal of Special Education,* Volume 37, Number 2, pp. 69–76

Woodcock, L and Page, A (2010) *Managing Family Meltdown.* London: Jessica Kingsley

Websites

Hand In Hand – the community in Ghana that cares for disabled children and adults, many of whom have ASC www.handinhanduk.org

Stephen Wiltshire – a very talented artist with autism www.stephenwiltshire.co.uk

I am often asked if I would like a cure for autism to be invented and I am aware that this is an area that generates a considerable amount of controversy. I have to admit to being torn between being an idealist and a pragmatist. In an ideal world, I would like to believe that the conditions would exist where people on the spectrum would be able to live lives as rewarding and fulfilling as neurotypicals. However, if I am brutally honest, I still believe we are a considerable way off this happening as a society, and I would be lying if I said there were occasions when I did not wish I could 'get rid' of my autism. I also think it's really important for both parents and individuals to be able to have a frank and open conversation about autism, and I have not met any carers or individuals who don't sometimes wish for a more neurotypical life. Whilst I understand that parents or carers may not wish to express this desire in front of their children, I do believe it is important for professionals to be sensitive to the fact that these feelings exist, and to help parents and carers understand and deal with these points of view. Similarly, people often ask me if the term 'sufferers' is appropriate in describing an individual on the spectrum. Whilst I would not say that my life is anywhere close to continuous suffering, I think it is vital for carers and professionals to understand the emotional pain that often comes as part of being an individual on the spectrum.

John

Introduction

There are many different theories and concepts about autism. It is important to find out about them as they will help you to better understand the people with autism that you know. The image of a jigsaw is often used in relation to autism and it is a useful one. For me it indicates that there are things we do know, which are like pieces of the jigsaw that we can put together. Then there are pieces being discovered through research that we can find out more about. However, there are also things that are currently not known, the missing pieces. So, we need to be aware of our own lack of knowledge and we need to find a way to keep up to date with new research and ideas.

In this chapter, we will look at some of the theories that have been well researched and that help to give us a clearer understanding of what autism is. Each of us needs to keep putting the pieces of the jigsaw together so that we can get a better insight into the whole puzzle that is autism.

Hearing from John about his personal experiences of living with autism is important. John is very able and his writings give us an insight into those people with autism who have additional learning disabilities, or those who are not able to be so self aware. There are a number of significant psychological theories that are linked specifically with autistic spectrum conditions and it is important to consider how these impact on people across the autistic spectrum.

Learning outcomes

This chapter will help you to:

- explain some of the significant theories about autism regarding brain function, genetics and psychology;
- explain why there are alternative choices of terminology used to describe the autism spectrum;
- describe the strengths and limitations of labels and different terminology;
- explain the contribution of autism rights groups and the implications of their views;
- outline the controversies regarding the search for cures and interventions for autism and for pre-natal diagnosis;
- describe why it is important to take account of individual differences about what is important in life.

Significant theories about autism regarding genetics, brain function and psychology

The genetics of autism

Many people want to know why they, a member of their family, or a friend has autism. Genetic testing may provide some of the answer, but it will not give them the whole answer. We do know that a person's genes play a significant part in the story about why they have autism. The twin and family studies carried out since the 1970s have indicated that there is a genetic component to autism, that is to say one part of the cause of a person's autism is that it was inherited from their parents. But this is not the whole story. Genetic research carried out over the last 20 years has indicated that there is no single gene associated with autism, rather there are a number of genes that are significantly more prevalent in people with autism.

But genetics do not fully account for the development of autism. Research currently indicates that there is usually a genetic component to a person's autism, together with a range of possible environmental factors that may trigger its development.

There is much more to be explored and understood in the area of genetics, environmental factors and autism, and at the end of this chapter you will be directed to further reading and resources.

Differences in brain function

The development of MRI scans (magnetic resonance imaging) has enabled the exploration of the functioning and development of the brain in children and adults with autism. These have indicated that the brains of children with autism develop differently to more neurotypical children and that when people with autism undertake particular tasks, certain areas of their brain function in a different way. These differences in the brain development and function of people with autism can help us to understand why they think and behave differently. Further studies are needed to fully understand the brain differences in people with autism and then how this understanding can help us to provide better support.

John is now very aware that his brain functions in a different way and that this affects the way he thinks. I have worked with many people with autism who do not have this level of self-awareness and as support workers we have to work hard at being one step ahead. We must always try and think in an autistic friendly way. We need to keep looking through an 'Asperger lens' as one individual suggests, or to ensure we have our 'autistic thinking hat' on when we come to work. This is the key to quality support for individuals with autism. It is a skill that all family carers and paid workers need to learn to develop and keep working on as they understand more about autistic spectrum conditions and more about the people they support. How often have you found yourself asking, 'Why does he do that?' Keep asking these kinds of questions, but in your answers try not to fall into the trap of answering them from a neurotypical perspective, by saying such things as:

- he does it to wind me up;

- she does it to get attention;

- he does it because he is rather selfish and always wants to get his own way;

- he is so manipulative.

All of these statements may appear to be true, but they are neurotypical assumptions. Consider the following two examples from staff teams I have been working with recently.

Example 1

When I come to work in a morning Roger always asks me the same question, 'How is your mum? Is your dad dead?'

I've tried to explain to him that it upsets me to be asked if my dad is dead. My dad died nearly a year ago now and at the time Roger was very interested. He used to ask, 'How's your mum?', then, 'How's your dad?' Instead he now asks every day 'Is your dad dead?' It is almost as if he does it on purpose to wind me up or upset me.

Staff member in a residential home for people with learning disabilities and autism

Example 2

We have six residents in the home. They all have autism and most of the time they seem to get on OK. There are just two who don't seem to like each other. We have a real problem because Gerald targets Sahail at times. It is a bit weird because Sahail will make this loud wailing nose that Gerald hates, but then Gerald does things to Sahail which prompt him to make the noise. He goes for him, really targets him and then doesn't like the result. We have tried to explain to Gerald, but so far the only way to stop it happening is to keep them apart.

Staff member in a residential home for people with learning disabilities and autism

The two examples above show staff assigning neurotypical brain function and ways of thinking to two individuals with autism. People with autism simply cannot think in this way.

Let us revisit the two examples.

Example 1 – Roger and the insensitive question

Roger does not know who is coming on shift and so each day he is very anxious about this. To help reduce his own anxiety, he has developed greeting patterns for each member of staff. These give him pleasure and time to process who has come to work with him that morning. These patterns help him begin to make sense of what the day will now be like. Last year, Charlotte's dad died and Roger was very confused at her reaction when she came to work and he greeted her with his normal greeting pattern, 'How's your mum? How's your dad?' He did not really understand what was said about Charlotte's dad being dead. However, he discovered that he got a better predictable pattern by asking, 'Is your dad dead?' which reduced his anxiety. So, Roger altered his greeting pattern to suit his own needs. It meant that every morning Charlotte was on shift, she was irritated and said, 'You know my dad is dead and you should not keep asking me this'. However, her response was now very familiar and the predictable pattern of words comforted Roger.

What should Charlotte do if she is thinking with her 'autistic hat' on? As an autism adviser I would suggest that she gives him the predictable response, 'Yes Roger, you know my dad is dead', but that she should also try to set up a more positive predictable greeting pattern with him. This will take time and effort but would be possible. It is the predictable response Roger is seeking and he is certainly not meaning to be annoying or insensitive.

Example 2 – Gerald and Sahail

We know that Sahail's wailing is a problem, because Gerald has very sensitive hearing. We also know that like most people with autism, Gerald likes things to be predictable. Not knowing when Sahail will make the wailing noise that he finds so painful is the cause of considerable anxiety for Gerald. He needs to know when the noise will happen in order for it to be less frightening. So, in his overwhelming need for predictability, as soon as Gerald sees Sahail he goes up to him and pokes him again and again until the wailing sound comes. Satisfied and slightly less anxious, Gerald then runs off with his fingers in his ears. He does not like the noise, but at least he is able to predict it is coming and this reduces Gerald's anxiety around Sahail.

It would be so easy for us to think that in both these cases we are dealing with individuals who are mean and vindictive. This is how their actions appear. But this is not the reality, and mistakenly seeing their behaviour from a neurotypical point of view means it is impossible to help. We must learn to think 'autistically' and to deal with issues in an autism friendly way. With Gerald and Sahail, as with Charlotte and Roger, the challenge is to help create positive predictable patterns. All too often, predictability for people with autism is negative and harmful. Individuals with autism want and need predictability and they strive hard to get it. The trouble is that if we are not supporting them to create more positive predictability it is likely to become negative, as in these two true stories. The longer behaviour goes on in this way, the harder it is to alter. We must always keep in mind the extreme high anxiety the majority of people with autism experience. Predictable patterns are a way for them to reduce those anxious feelings. Our challenge as support staff is to make the predictable patterns in their lives more positive ones.

Thinking point

Have you been, or are you now, part of a negative predictable pattern with someone with autism that you support?

Activity

Consider a behaviour of someone with autism that you know and that you find challenging. Try to think about it from a more autistic view point. When you do this does the possible reason for the behaviour seem different? If so, maybe your response to the behaviour needs to be different.

Significant psychological theories in autistic spectrum conditions

As we look at these theories you need to remember that they are not the cause of a person's autism, but rather they explain some of the effects of having an autistic spectrum condition. It is also important to note that they are theories that are still being researched and tested. The three we will look at here are the most currently accepted and understood, as it is important that if we are to support people with autism well we must also have some knowledge and understanding about the psychological effects of autism.

Theory of mind

John helps us again here by sharing some of his own personal experiences that he is now able to reflect on. Below, he gives us two stories to consider that relate to what is called 'theory of mind'. Theory of mind is the ability to know and understand that other people may think differently to you. It is also the ability to empathise.

John says:

Whilst eating a Sunday roast at my Gran's house once, I remember being confused by the things my parents were saying about the dinner being 'tasty' and the meat we were eating being a 'nice piece of beef'. I was finding it very difficult to eat because it was tough and I could not chew it. I could not understand why mum and dad were saying these things and in the end blurted out, 'Are we eating the same piece of meat? Mine is awful!' Mum and dad were not happy with me which again did not make sense to me.

Now I know they were being polite, which meant they in effect told a lie. If I am honest I still find this confusing but I know it is something that people do.

On 11 September 2001, when there was the terrorist attack on the twin towers in New York, I came home from school and was looking forward to the Champions' League football that was going to be on TV. When I saw that there was nothing on apart from news about these terrorist attacks I was anxious, upset and cross. My parents seemed distressed about what was on the news and this didn't make sense to me either. I needed MY football and at the time had no ability to empathise with what had happened or with how even my parents were feeling about it.

I am older now and have learnt a great deal about my own autism and the impact it has on all aspects of my life and the way my mind works. I still find it very difficult to work out what other people may think or why they are not thinking about buses and football all the time like me, but I have a little more awareness now and with help and guidance can begin to understand how other people might think and feel. This is not easy for me but I try very hard.

The consequences for people with autism of having a poor theory of mind are hard for support workers and others to understand. Family members and workers may get abused verbally or physically and it is very difficult to try and accept that the individual who has hurt you has little or no understanding of how you think and feel. I am not saying that people with autistic spectrum conditions never know or understand that they may have hurt someone. Rather, I am suggesting that the lack of theory of mind can certainly mean this *at times*. It is worth reading more about theory of mind in order to understand it as much as possible. Then consider your understanding in relation to those with autism you work with. An excellent resource for learning more in this area is a book by Ilona Roth, *The Autism Spectrum in the 21st Century* (2010).

Another good example comes from a very able individual with Asperger syndrome whom I know. She once told me how it never occurred to her when she was at school that the messages and notes she was given for her parents needed to be passed on to them. She often got into trouble for not passing notes on, but she kept failing to do so. She could not understand why her parents did not know about the information in the notes – she had read them and knew so why didn't they? Now she knows her parents did not share her thoughts and knowledge and her assumptions were due to her poor theory of mind.

Thinking point

When do young children first begin to be aware of what others think and feel? If their mum answered the phone one day and began to cry because she was given some sad news, what would a typically developing two year old do? Cry as well? Give mum a cuddle? Either of these is very likely because at this time a child's theory of mind is developing. They are able to grasp that something is happening with mum and it won't be long before they are able to show genuine empathy.

Activity

Discuss theory of mind with one of your colleagues, in relation to the behaviour of the individuals you work with. What kind of theory of mind do you think they really have? How able are they to understand other people's thoughts?

There are two other psychological theories which we are going to explore briefly:

- executive function;
- central coherence.

Executive function

Executive function is about an ability to plan, to shift attention, to inhibit responses and to generate new ideas of things to do. People with autism often have poor executive functioning skills. This is an area that it would be good to learn more about so that you can better understand the people you support. Let's consider this and its impact for John.

> *John says:*
>
> I know now that I have poor executive function – I just can't organise or plan things like what to wear, when clothes are dirty, what I will need when I go to work. Mum does so much thinking for me and people don't realise. I know that this can make me appear lazy and at times it really frustrates my parents but I just can't work these things out, or even the fact that there is a need to work them out.

Visual supports can help people to plan their time.

Working out how long it takes to do things is an executive functioning skill. It is an executive function that enables you to adapt the next time when you discover it takes longer than you thought to get a bus from home to college. For someone with autism, without good help and support, it is likely that they will keep being late, as they will keep getting the same bus, rather than being able to make the decision to catch an earlier one if this meant a change in routine.

For someone who may have severe learning disabilities and autism this may mean difficulties in following a simple morning routine in the right order without support. We might think they should learn the order that clothes go on and be surprised and a little frustrated if they put their jumper on and then try to put on their t-shirt which was meant to go on underneath. However, with the right kind of support this problem can be overcome by making the routine visual.

There is much more to learn about executive function and what it means for people with autistic spectrum conditions. Currently research is continuing to explore this further. Paula Johnston (2004), in a book which she and I wrote together, explains how hard she finds it to make a cup of tea. She needs to practice the same routine over and over again in order to be able to carry out some quite simple tasks and yet she is a highly intelligent woman. She also explains about an administrative job she had that involved a series of simple tasks, which she wrote down when they were first explained to her. She stuck the list of instructions on the wall next to her desk. For several weeks Paula carried out this job. After a few weeks a new supervisor arrived who felt that the list on the wall was unnecessary and insisted that it came down. For Paula this was the end of her being able to do the job and carry out the tasks and after a tearful afternoon she was sent home and replaced by another admin temp.

Thinking point

What do you do to help you complete a task in the right order and to plan ahead? Could these ideas be adapted in an autism friendly way to support those you work with?

Activity

Try using a visual support to help an individual with autism you work with to carry out a task more independently. If it works, keep using it and don't try to take it away too quickly.

Central coherence

The theory of weak central coherence is about how many people with autistic spectrum conditions seem to focus on the details in a situation or an object and not see the whole picture. Elizabeth's son Edward (whom I speak about a lot in the previous book in this series, *An Introduction to Supporting People with Autistic Spectrum Conditions*), loves to spin wheels on cars, on his buggy when he was small and on any toy with a wheel. He seems to be uninterested and unaware of the whole object and what it can do – the actual wheels are the only focus for him. Many of you will know of individuals with autism who seem to know instantly if something has been moved in their room or who will go to straighten an ornament at Grandma's house. It is this attention to detail that draws their focus and not the delicious tea that Grandma has prepared for them, set out on the table.

Until recently this has been seen as a deficit and a real problem for people with autism. However, there is now a view that such focus could be seen as a strength. The ability to concentrate so keenly on one thing and to have an acute eye for detail can be a valued skill if it is put to the right use. It is this aspect of autism that leads to some people being amazingly gifted in certain areas such as music or mathematics. It is certainly this ability to focus on detail that gives Stephen Wiltshire his amazing talent for drawing buildings and cityscapes.

There is more to learn and more to be discovered about central coherence and autism. I have no doubt that John's ability to focus on the detail of a bus timetable is very valuable when you are trying to work out which bus to catch and where it stops. He is the person you would want with you if you were making a complicated journey by bus, although he may well forget the bigger picture of why we might be getting on the bus.

Thinking point

In what kind of situation is paying extreme attention to detail a really valuable skill?

Activity

Consider a person with autism you know well. Do they pay particular attention to details? Is this seen as a problem? Could it be used as a strength? Discuss this with a friend or colleague.

The strengths and limitations of different labels and terminology

There is a great deal of discussion and debate about the different labels used for people with autistic spectrum conditions. Labels come from the criteria that are used to give a diagnosis but in addition from use in everyday situations and research. We will begin by considering some of the labels and then think about how useful they are.

We need first of all to remind ourselves of the two classification systems used by medical professionals, The Diagnostic and Statistical Manual of Mental Disorders (DSM-IV) and the International Classification of Diseases (ICD-10). These were developed by the American Psychiatric Association and the World Health Organisation. The diagnostic criteria are reviewed and updated periodically and both are going through this process at the time of writing. It is expected that there will be the new DSM (DSM-V) out in 2013, and a new ICD (ISC-11) out in 2015, so there is lots of work going on to ensure that these classification systems are as accurate as possible. Currently within the DSM-IV there are distinct types of pervasive developmental disorders including the following:

- Autistic disorder – difficulties in three main areas: social interaction, communication and repetitive and restrictive behaviours.

- Asperger disorder – the behaviours are almost identical to those described for a diagnosis of autistic disorder, though some are more subtle. (For example, John will tell you he flaps, but he does it in his pocket with a piece of card rather than in front of his eyes. He still finds this action calming.)

- Pervasive developmental disorder not otherwise specified (PDD-NOS, sometimes known as atypical autism) – this is used for those who almost meet the full criteria for autism but not quite.

As well as these, you may also have heard of the term 'classic autism' or 'Kanner's autism' used in addition to 'autistic spectrum disorder', and, as we are using in this book, 'autistic spectrum conditions'. It was a doctor called Leo Kanner who described autism in the 1940s, when he was working with children who had what we would now describe as severe learning disabilities as well as autism. Children who present in a similar way today are often referred to as having Kanner's, or classic autism. The term autistic spectrum disorder, or autistic spectrum conditions, was developed in the early 1980s by the British psychiatrist Dr Lorna Wing (1996).

One of the key distinctions about receiving a diagnosis for Asperger syndrome is around the development of language. Children with Asperger syndrome meet the usual milestones for their language development, which means that getting a diagnosis often happens much later than for those with other autistic spectrum conditions, whose language development is impaired.

Another term you may hear being used is 'high functioning autism', which is often used to describe somebody who does not have an Asperger syndrome diagnosis but who has an autistic spectrum condition and is very able. This term is not part of the official classification systems.

Does it matter about the label? Some will say that, if you have autism, you have autism and a more generic term may stop confusion and unite those campaigning for good support. However, there are those for whom the label is very important because it brings with it certain attitudes and reactions from other people in the community. The new criteria that are to be published soon are likely to clarify some of this confusion and stick with the diagnosis of being on the autism spectrum.

John says, about his own diagnosis:

When I first heard the word autism being used about me, I thought the staff at the CAMHS (child and adolescent mental health service) were talking nonsense. All I knew about autism, or all I thought I knew, was that people with the condition did not speak and spent all day rocking. How could that apply to me? The term Asperger syndrome did not mean anything really until I began to get to know people in a local Asperger discussion group. Then I began to see what the label meant and how the individuals in the group were like me – very like me. I learnt we were actually all autistic, although many of us hold down a job and cope in a fairly independent way.

I now tend to talk of myself as having autism because I think it is easier to use one label for the broad overarching condition. It helps to get across to people the concept of a spectrum. There is a real danger that you think people like me, who are what you might call 'high functioning' because I am clever in lots of ways and was a high achiever in school in many subjects (but not all), do not have all the difficulties that come with having an autistic spectrum condition. Although I can appear to be coping well, I still struggle with so many things that are easy for neurotypical people to understand and do. Likewise with some of the guys I support in the home where I work part time as a support worker.

They are labelled as having autism with severe learning disabilities and yet there are some things that they are very good at. The important thing is to have a good understanding of what the label autism covers and how it affects people differently and yet also in a similar way. I think all the different labels can be confusing.

It is likely that the term Asperger syndrome will not be in the new diagnostic criteria and some people think this could prove controversial. I suspect it will continue to be used, not least by the Asperger community across the world, who are now very much in touch with each other via the internet and doing their best to advocate for themselves.

Thinking point

Do you think it is important to have a label and if so why?

Activity

Try and talk to someone with a diagnosis of Asperger syndrome or autism who is able, and willing to let you know what they think and feel about the various labels. If this is not possible, try to read something by an individual with an autistic spectrum condition and see what they have to say about the various labels and the possible changes with the new DSM-V due in 2013.

The contribution of autism rights groups

A growing number of groups are seeking to speak out for the rights of people with autistic spectrum conditions. One of the first organisations in the UK to become the voice of families was the National Autistic Society (NAS), of which Dr Lorna Wing was a founder member. The NAS continues to have a campaigning arm as well as providing a wide range of services. There has always been a considerable involvement from parents and family members speaking up for individuals with autism and since there is more understanding of the nature of the spectrum of autism there are now lots of individuals with a diagnosis involved at many levels within the NAS. Many national, regional and local autistic societies also involve people on the spectrum to ensure that the voice of those with autism is heard. For some individuals, these groups do not go far enough. They are seen to be dominated by people who do not have a diagnosis and therefore do not adequately understand the needs and aspirations of people with autistic spectrum conditions.

One organisation that has been running for a number of years now is Autscape (www.autscape.org). Each year, Autscape run a three day conference for people with autism and the whole event is run by people on the spectrum. Through this they aim to empower those who attend. Although Autscape itself is not a political campaigning group, there are those who meet there who have set up or are involved with other organisations that are more politically active. The London Autistic Rights Movement is one such organisation seeking to promote 'Nothing about aUtiSm without aUtiStics'.

It is important for those of us who work in the field to listen to these able and articulate people who have a diagnosis of autism. Everyone on the spectrum is different and the way their autistic spectrum condition impacts upon each person's life is also different. Listening to an individual can give us a valuable insight that as neurotypical people we cannot find for ourselves, no matter how well we feel we have got to know someone. Self-awareness and self-understanding is one area that I feel is a particular challenge for families and professionals. In the last 16 years I have worked with a wide range of people with autism to help them understand themselves and in every case the outcome has been very positive for the individual. They may go through periods of not being happy with the things they discover, but overall it helps them to make sense of themselves. As family members and workers I think we all too often shy away from finding ways of helping people understand their own diagnosis and why they do, say and feel the things they do. The autism rights movement is interesting and challenging in this respect. It will make you think and ask, 'What can I do to help someone I support understand themselves better?' It may be that the person you support has severe learning disabilities and autism, but self-awareness work is as important for them as it is for the person with a diagnosis of Asperger syndrome. Without the right support to aid self-awareness, individuals can never understand what impact they are having, on themselves and others.

There are now lots of materials published to help in the development of self-awareness and also a great many personal accounts of living with autism. John has an interesting contribution to make when considering advocacy, rights and self-knowledge.

> *John says:*
>
> One of the issues that I consider to be the most challenging concerning autism is the level to which individuals on the spectrum act as good self advocates. Because we struggle to see the world from anyone else's viewpoint and tend to be very single minded and dominated by our special interests, I do feel we need the guidance of those we can trust who will have our best interests at heart. I know I need to learn to listen to them as much as they need to learn to listen to me.

There may well be those within the autism rights movement who might disagree with John, but he has come to this decision after a number of years working at understanding himself. During these years those who live with and support John have had to do considerable learning as well. The NAS slogan for the year 2000 was 'Understanding makes a difference'. Understanding, in terms of thinking 'autistically' and in terms of supporting self awareness, is paramount.

Thinking point

How much self awareness do the people you support have of their own autistic spectrum condition? What can you do to improve this?

Activity

Have a look on the internet at the websites for the various autism rights groups and talk about what you find with a colleague. Ask yourself if there is something you can learn from these websites to guide you in helping people with autism to develop increased self awareness and understanding.

Controversies regarding cures, pre-natal diagnosis and interventions for autism

Over the years there have been people who say that they have recovered from autism, and even some who would say there is a cure. I think it is important to understand these claims, but then to look at the body of evidence and scientific research across the world that would say that autistic spectrum condition is a pervasive developmental disorder which is impossible to 'cure'.

By getting the support and the education right for people diagnosed with autism it is possible to greatly reduce the negative impact of their condition. As I often say to those I work with, the autism is not going away, but if we understand it well we can make a positive difference to the lives of people and their families.

Once, I listened to a person who claimed to be a 'recovered autistic'. The experience made me angry, because a large number of parents I knew, who had children who were severely autistic, were listening to him. I felt that raising the hopes, in this way, of parents, a group who were sometimes vulnerable and distressed, was wrong. Whilst it is important to look closely at the wide range of interventions available, the most reliable theories and research would discourage any notion of a 'cure'.

We are now able to identify autism much earlier in children, which means that families and professionals can begin to work in more autism friendly ways much earlier. However, it will still be some time before autism can be identified at the pre- or post-natal stage. Families that already have a child with autism will be watching closely the development of any subsequent siblings and other extended family members. They will be keen to do all they can to lessen the negative impact of an autistic spectrum condition on a child.

In terms of interventions that work for people with autism, much has been written about different approaches. Glenys Jones (2002) offers us a valuable list of interventions that form part of a developing body of evidence about what works for children and young people. These include:

- intervene early;

- involve parents;

- create an environment that is sensitive to sensory difficulties;

- develop joint attention and communication skills;

- allow sufficient time for information processing;

- gain information on the individual's view of what is offered;

- use the individual's special interests and skills and include activities that he or she enjoys;

- take account of the differences between individuals with an autistic spectrum condition;

- support transitions;

- take a long term perspective;
- provide regular exercise;
- give training in relaxation.

When talking with a person with autism allow sufficient time for information processing.

That list was written some time ago, but it holds true today. I would be a little more explicit about the value of visual supports in lots of different ways and also stress the value of developing self-awareness where possible.

I once asked 40 people who were either on the autism spectrum themselves, parents of someone on the spectrum or professionals with a lot of experience in the field, what they felt were the five most important things to get right when working or living with someone with an autistic spectrum condition. I was amazed by the similarity of the answers. Their top five interventions were:

1. Create a calm atmosphere.

2. Have an uncluttered environment.

3. Use visual support to aid communication.

4. Have a good structure to a meaningful (to them) day.

5. Ensure real engagement between staff or family member and the individual with autism.

Create a calm atmosphere.

Time and time again I meet people with autism who are anxious and challenging due to their environment. With the right interventions to address the points above, they have dramatically reduced their anxiety and become more contented and happy people. It is not about cure, but rather it is about using the wealth of knowledge that is out there, so that those with autistic spectrum conditions are able to live more fulfilled and rewarding lives.

Thinking point

What do you contribute to ensure the atmosphere is calm and uncluttered for the people with autism that you support?

Think about where you work, and talk to a colleague about the five points above and the suggestions of interventions that work. What score out of ten would you give your place of work for following these suggestions?

Taking account of individual differences about what is important in life

People with autism are individuals and have their own personalities. They grow up in different families and cultures which also effect who they are. Then they have an autistic spectrum condition, and the ways this impacts on them varies, as we have established. They may also have other associated conditions that complicate their life further. Our task, if we are to be good practitioners in this field, is to develop our understanding of autistic spectrum conditions. Learn about the spectrum and what the diagnostic criteria mean. Then begin to explore what that diagnosis means for each individual.

You can do this by profiling THEIR autism, their communication difficulties, their sensory issues, their gifts and skills. In doing this, and trying each day we come to work, to think in an autistic friendly way, we really will make a difference to the lives of those we support. It is not easy to do this and I believe we have to make a conscious effort to think and work in this way on a regular basis. As neurotypical individuals, thinking in an autism friendly way does not come naturally no matter how long we have worked in the field. So we have to make the effort and the rewards will be worth it as we see people calm down and enabled to participate in life in ways they find rewarding.

Key points from this chapter

- People with autism have brains that work in different ways to neurotypical people.

- Our task is to learn to think in more autism friendly ways and then to work with a more autism aware approach.

- People with autism may appear to be something they are not and we need to learn not to make assumptions but to get to know the person and THEIR autism well.

References and where to go for more information

References

Hatton, S and Johnston, P (2004) *Conversations in Autism.* BILD: Kidderminster

Jones, G (2002) *Educational Provision for Children with Autism and Asperger Syndrome.* London: David Fulton

National Autistic Society (2008) *Being Me. A self-development resource pack for people on the autism spectrum (DVD).* London: National Autistic Society

Pike, R (2008) *Talking Together about an Autism Diagnosis.* London: National Autistic Society

Roth, I (2010) *The Autism Spectrum in the 21st Century.* London: Jessica Kingsley

Wing, L (2003) *The Autistic Spectrum.* London: Robinson Publishers

Websites

Autscape www.autscape.org

London Autistic Rights Movement (LARM) www.larmuk.webs.com

Chapter 4

Understanding the legal and policy framework that underpins good practice

The Autism Act 2010 was a unique and groundbreaking piece of legislation. It signalled a new commitment across government to transferring the ways public services support adults with autism… The national autism strategy – the first ever created in England – is the next major landmark in this process… Above all, the strategy seeks to put the needs of adults with autism on the map in every area, so that throughout England the right services can be developed, commissioned and shaped to meet those needs.

Fulfilling and Rewarding Lives. The Strategy for Adults with Autism in England (Department of Health, 2010)

The Department (the Department of Health, Social Services and Public Safety) must prepare a strategy on autism to be known as the autism strategy and must publish the autism strategy in no less than two years after the passing of this Act…

The autism strategy must set out how the needs of persons with autism are to be addressed throughout their lives…

The autism strategy must set out how the needs of families and carers of persons with autism are to be addressed…

Autism Act (Northern Ireland) 2011

The Scottish Government will provide strategic leadership on improving the lives of people affected by autism. It will lead on creating a strategic vision for the development of services and support for people with autism, their families and carers.

The Scottish Strategy for Autism 2011

> The purpose of this Strategic Action Plan is to set a clear direction of travel for the development of services in Wales by ensuring that specific and measurable actions are undertaken and, on the basis of evidence of prevalence and need, commissioning interagency services at local, regional or national levels as appropriate. It also aims to broaden our understanding of ASD (autistic spectrum disorders) and its prevalence in Wales
>
> *ASD Strategic Action Plan for Wales (2008)*

Introduction

Many workers don't have time to consider the legal and policy framework that affects their day to day work. Often people say they are too busy getting on with the job, but you need to know about the legal framework because a range of laws impact on what you do.

In recent years, each of the four UK countries has developed strategies or legislation to address the inclusion and support for individuals with autism. This is largely due to the recognition that individuals on the spectrum do not fit easily into the categories of learning disability or mental health that had previously sought to meet their needs. A range of other legislation, such as the Human Rights Act (1998), the Equality Act (2010) and the legislation on mental capacity, also has relevance for individuals on the spectrum. Statutory guidance specific to people with autistic spectrum conditions is essential if high quality support is to be consistently provided.

In this chapter, we will look at some of the general and specific legislation and guidance that relates to adults with autism and explore how it can support staff to work effectively. In addition, we explain the opportunities it can give individuals and their families to ensure they receive the right support.

Legislation, policies and guidance that applies to people on the autistic spectrum

UK autism legislation and policies

In recent years the governments in the four UK countries have been lobbied effectively by people with autism, family carers and leading charities concerned about the lack of support for people on the spectrum. Each of the individual governments has now recognised the need for either legislation or a national strategic plan to shape and direct the development of services and support in the future. The table below provides a summary of the laws and guidance relating to people on the spectrum in England, Northern Ireland, Scotland and Wales. You can get an up-to-date picture from the website www.legislation. gov.uk

Country	Name of document/s and summary of content	Published by
ENGLAND	The Autism Act 2009, the first ever disability-specific law in England. It put a duty on the government to produce a strategy for adults with autism; *Fulfilling and Rewarding Lives. The Strategy for Adults with Autism in England* was published on 2 March 2010. The strategy placed a duty on the government to produce statutory guidance for local councils and local health bodies on implementing the adult autism strategy by the end of 2010. This guidance was published on 17 December 2010.	Department of Health www.dh.gov.uk
SCOTLAND	In 2008 Scotland produced *Commissioning Services for People on the Autism Spectrum: Policy and Practice Guidance* to inform those commissioning health and social care services for people with autism. In 2010 *Towards an Autism Strategy for Scotland* was published for consultation. *The Scottish Strategy for Autism* was launched in 2011.	The Scottish Government www.scotland.gov.uk
NORTHERN IRELAND	The Autism Act (Northern Ireland) was passed in 2011. It states that the Department of Health, Social Services and Public Safety has to prepare a strategy on autism that must be published in not less than two years after the passing of this Act.	Northern Ireland Assembly and Parliament www.legislation.gov.uk www.niassembly.gov.uk
WALES	*The Autistic Spectrum Disorder (ASD) Strategic Action Plan for Wales* was launched in 2008. This was the first time guidelines specific to autism and Asperger syndrome were set out for local authorities to follow in Wales. The plan also outlines what the Welsh Government has to do in order to meet the needs of people with autism and their families. It covers everyone on the autism spectrum in Wales, including people with Asperger syndrome.	Welsh Government www.wales.gov.uk

All of the above legislation focuses on adults with autism. If you are supporting children or young people in an educational or care environment there are many other pieces of legislation that may be relevant. You can find out more on the National Autistic Society website at www.autism.org.uk

Activity

Read through the national laws or guidance about supporting people with autism that relates to the country that you work in. Then look at the mission statement, aims and objectives of your organisation. Do these relate to the national policies?

Other UK legislation and policies that promote human rights, inclusion and citizenship of people with autism

There are three main pieces of national legislation you need to know about when supporting people with autistic spectrum conditions. These are:

- the Human Rights Act 1998;

- the Mental Capacity Act 2005 (England and Wales) or the Adults with Incapacity (Scotland) Act 2000;

- the Equality Act 2010.

You will also need to know how the policies and procedures of your organisation reflect and implement the legislation. If you work as a personal assistant directly employed by a person with autism and/or their family carers, there may not be the policies and procedures that you would find in an organisation. Your contract of employment and the agreed ways of working that your employer discusses with you will form the basis of how you should work. Wherever you work, you need to know about these key laws on equality, rights and inclusion and how they should underpin your day to day practice.

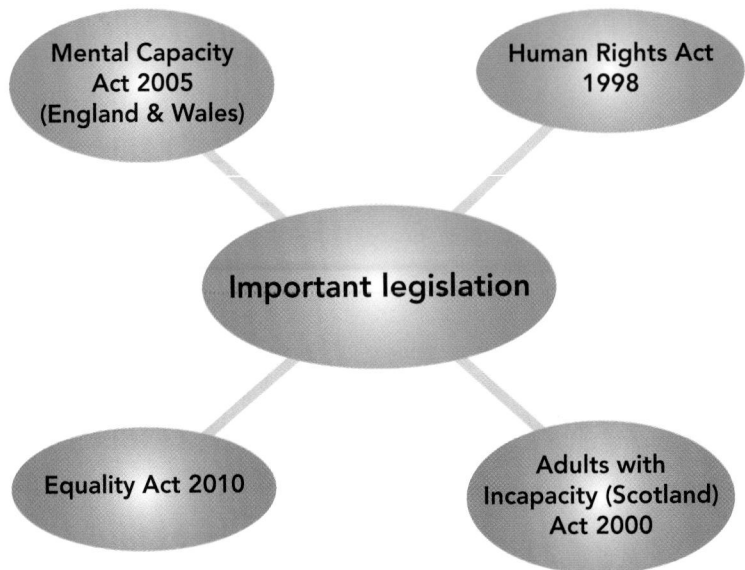

The Human Rights Act 1998

One of the most important laws for you to get to know and understand is the Human Rights Act 1998. Human rights are based on the following core values:

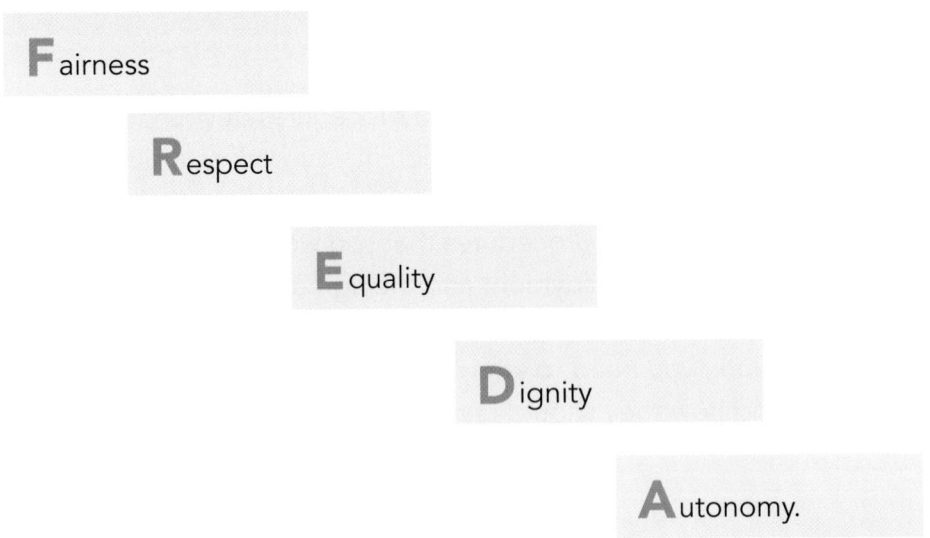

Fairness

Respect

Equality

Dignity

Autonomy.

These are often called the FREDA values. The Human Rights Act requires public authorities in the UK – including the government, hospitals and social services – to treat people with fairness, equality, dignity and respect. The act provides a legal framework within which service providers must operate, and at the same time a legal framework within which individuals can demand to be treated with respect for their dignity. In this way, the Human Rights Act (HRA) provides each of us with a powerful means of protection against discrimination and injustice. The Act is especially important for people with autism as it includes:

- the right not to be tortured or treated in an inhuman or degrading way (article 3);

- the right to respect for private and family life, home and correspondence (article 8);

- the right to life (article 2);

- the right to liberty (article 5);

- the right not to be discriminated against (article 14).

The HRA says that all providers of public services must make sure they do not breach the human rights of people with disabilities. Here, 'providers of public services' include people working in residential homes and day services as well as workers who support people in their own home. An important part of your job is keeping in mind the human rights of the individual you are supporting in everything that you do. You may also need to stand up for their human rights.

Activity

Discuss the FREDA values at your next supervision or team meeting and ask your colleagues how your organisation promotes these values when supporting people with autism.

The Mental Capacity Act 2005

The Mental Capacity Act (MCA) is an important law for people with autism in England and Wales and one that you need to know and understand clearly if you are to support people effectively. (In Scotland you should refer to the Adults with Incapacity (Scotland) Act 2000; in Northern Ireland mental health issues are currently dealt with under common law although there are plans to introduce capacity legislation.) The Mental Capacity Act provides a legal framework for making choices and decisions for people aged 16 or over who are unable to make such decisions themselves. The kind of decisions the MCA covers includes decisions relating to health, welfare, finance and property.

Activity

Find out more about the capacity legislation in your country, and how it relates to the lives of the people with autism that you support. If possible, go on a training day about capacity issues. Share what you find out at a supervision or team meeting.

The MCA says that people have capacity unless it can be shown that they cannot make their own decisions. This is important for people with autistic spectrum conditions because people might presume they do not have capacity.

> [I]t should be assumed that an adult (aged 16 or over) has full legal capacity to make decisions for themselves (the right to autonomy) unless it can be shown that they lack capacity to make a decision for themselves at the time that the decision needs to be made. *(MCA 2005, Code of Practice, 1.2)*

The MCA also says that an individual can only be treated as unable to make a decision if all practical steps to help them make the decision have been taken. When the person is judged to lack capacity to make that particular decision, the decision which is made for them must be made in their best interests and also in a way that is least restricting of their rights and freedom of action.

There are five key principles that underpin the Mental Capacity Act. These are:

1. All adults are presumed to have capacity to make decisions.

2. A person may only be treated as unable to make a decision if all practical steps to help them make the decision have been taken.

3. Any decision made on the person's behalf must be made in their best interests after a sharing of views by people who know the person well, for example their family and friends, workers who have known them a long time.

4. Any decision made on the person's behalf must be made in a way that is least restricting of their rights and freedom of action.

5. A person who lacks capacity and has no family or friends who would be appropriate to ask about important decisions should be represented and supported by an advocate.

It is important to support people to make choices and decisions in an autism friendly way.

Activity

Find out from your line manager about the arrangements in your organisation for supporting people with assessing capacity and decision making. Also find out how family carers are involved and whether they have access to any information to support their involvement in making a best interest decision.

The Equality Act 2010

The Equality Act 2010 brings together all of the previous laws about discrimination in Britain. (In Northern Ireland, which is not covered by the Equality Act, people will have less protection against unlawful discrimination, harassment and victimisation until the law there is changed.) The Equality Act provides legal protection against discrimination under six equality 'strands':

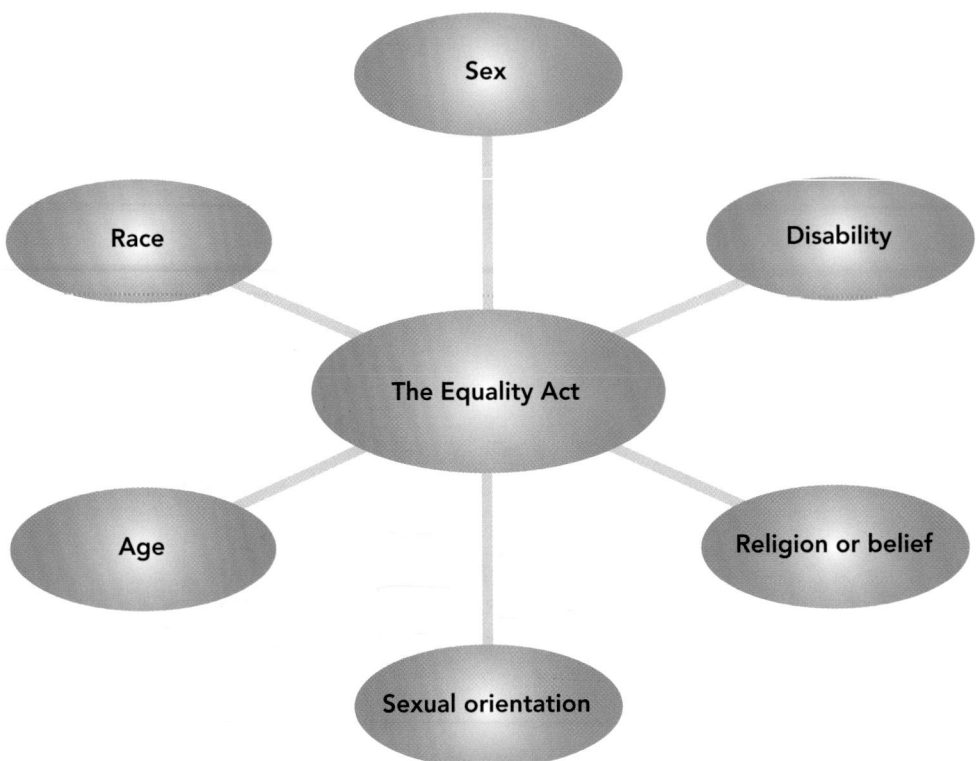

- sex;
- race;
- disability;
- age;
- religion or belief;
- sexual orientation.

In terms of disability discrimination, the Equality Act 2010 replaces the Disability Discrimination Acts 1995 and 2005. For people with autism and those who support them, the Act also introduces the following changes.

- It protects a person from being discriminated against because they are linked to or associated with a person with disabilities. This new protection could be important for family carers and for support workers. It would make it unlawful for a business or service provider to discriminate against either a family carer or a member of staff because they are with, or associated with, a person or people with a disability.

- Direct discrimination against people with disabilities is now unlawful, not only in the workplace, but when individuals are accessing goods and services. For example, a pub or restaurant cannot now refuse to serve a person because of their need for support to eat on the grounds that it will put others off their food.

- It is unlawful to discriminate against an individual because of something connected with their disability. This is called discrimination arising from disability. An example would be telling a man with a hearing impairment that he cannot not stay in a hotel because he would not be able to hear the fire alarm.

- It is now unlawful to cause indirect discrimination. This is putting in place a rule or way of doing things that has a worse impact on someone with a 'protected characteristic' such as autism than someone without one, when this cannot be justified.

- Disability harassment is now unlawful. This is when someone's behaviour violates a person with a disability's dignity or creates an environment for them that is intimidating, hostile, degrading, humiliating or offensive. For example, calling someone names or bullying them because they have a disability.

You can get more information about the Equality Act from the Equality and Human Rights Commission at www.equalityhumanrights.com and in the book *Equality and Inclusion for Learning Disability Workers* by Rorie Fulton and Kate Richardson in this series.

Other important policies and legislation
Safeguarding adults

Research shows that people with autism are more likely to suffer abuse than other members of society. This is for a wide range of reasons including: not realising that they are being abused; not being able to communicate with others about what is happening to them; or their dependence on their abuser. It is the responsibility of everyone who works with people with autism to be aware that abuse happens and know what to do if they think that it is happening.

Safeguarding adults, or protection of vulnerable adults as it used to be called, is an important policy that will be found in your workplace. This will tell you about the signs of potential abuse so that you can recognise them and know what to do.

This policy is based on a number of national policies and legislation, with each of the four nations of the UK each having their own version. These include:

- No Secrets (2000) was the first English government guidance to address the protection of vulnerable adults. It explains that all professionals must work together when safeguarding people. Every care service in your local authority area will also follow the same procedure to make sure that everyone works in the same way.

- Safeguarding Vulnerable Groups Act (2006) (England) has introduced the new Independent Safeguarding Authority (ISA), which means that everyone working with vulnerable adults will need to be registered with the ISA to work within this area. This is an extra safeguard to ensure that people who are abusers cannot have access to the most vulnerable people within society.

- The Adult Support and Protection (Scotland) Act 2007 and the Protection of Vulnerable Groups (Scotland) Act 2007, and The Safeguarding Vulnerable Groups Act 2006 (Controlled Activity) (Wales) Regulations 2010 provide the safeguards to protect vulnerable adults, including people with autism.

Confidentiality

It is important to recognise that people with autism deserve the respect and privacy that we expect for ourselves, and that their personal information must be kept confidential. Your workplace will have a policy about confidentiality – this is to make sure you know what information you can or cannot share, and with which people and when you can share it.

The Data Protection Act (2003) covers the UK and sets out the rules for how any information held about an individual should be used in a lawful way. This Act tells you how you handle confidential information about any person that you support. There is more information about this Act in the book, *Handling Information for Learning Disability Workers* by Lesley Barcham and Jackie Pountney in this series.

Applying the legislation and policies to people with autism

Organisational policies and procedures

The policies and procedures of the organisation that you work for should be directly informed by the legislation and guidance for the country that you work in.

When you start a new job, you should receive induction training during which you are made aware of your organisation's policies and procedures. If you work as a personal assistant you will also receive induction training and you should find out from your employer whether they have policies and procedures for staff or if they have agreed the ways that you should support them, for example through a contract of employment or supervision.

If you feel you do not understand the policies and procedures, or agreed ways of working, or you need more information about your role and responsibilities, talk to your line manager about it in supervision. Don't be afraid to ask questions as it is important you know and understand what to do if you have concerns.

Local policies

As you can see from the information above, the current state of guidance and legislation can be confusing. However, the legislation for individuals with autism differs only slightly according to where they live. What is clear is that England, Northern Ireland, Scotland and Wales are all developing similar legislation on autism that will ensure that statutory guidance is in place for local authorities in all parts of the UK. This will mean that local authorities will have to collect data about the people in their area with autism, and they will have to provide support and services. Currently in England the statutory guidance requires that each local authority and NHS service:

- should provide autism awareness training for all staff;
- must provide specialist autism training for key staff, such as GPs and community care assessors;
- cannot refuse a community care assessment for adults with autism based solely on IQ;
- must appoint an autism lead in their area;
- have to develop a clear pathway to diagnosis and assessment for adults with autism;
- must commission services based on adequate population data.

Some local authorities are developing their required approach to satisfy the guidance of the autism strategy quicker than others. For example, the strategy states that the 'Director of Adult Social Services (DASS) should ensure there is a joint commissioner/senior manager who has in his/her portfolio a clear commissioning responsibility for adults with autism' (6.10). The National Autistic Society website has a useful list of contact details for all those local authorities with a lead manager in place (for more information on this go to www.autism.org.uk). In time, the standards of provision for everybody with autistic spectrum conditions should be vastly improved, as resources are directed to increasing knowledge and improving services.

John's experience and that of his family might have been different if he was entering the adolescent psychiatric ward today. We know this as five years ago John and his mother and I were invited to deliver training for the range of staff working in the Child and Adolescent Mental Health Services (CAMHS) service. There was a recognition and acknowledgement of the real lack of understanding of autism for this group of staff, which was echoed in the National Autistic Society's campaign regarding the needs of children with autism within CAMHS services. This campaign was followed in 2011 by the publication of *Difference in Mind: Scrutinising Child and Adolescent Mental Health Services for Children with Autism*, by the Centre for Public Scrutiny.

A quote from the report reinforces the need for staff in mental health services to receive appropriate training:

> With the right support, at the right time, many of these problems can be prevented. But where mental health problems do develop, because autism is a complex disability, these problems are harder to recognise, harder to evaluate and harder to treat.

John says:

I was really pleased to be invited back to the unit I was on for six months, even though it felt a little strange. The staff team who attended the training were really committed to a better understanding of autism and during the five days that they committed to this training many connections were made with the young people that they had on the wards at the time and many they had treated previously, including myself of course. Every member of the course said training in autism was essential for all CAMHS staff. In many ways, these were a very forward thinking team when you consider the legislation and guidance that has followed.

Each part of the UK now has guidance about working with individuals with autism. However, it often takes time to filter down from government to the front line work of staff in local authorities and support providers. Parents, advocates and individuals themselves will need to continue to lobby and ensure that the professionals are supported by knowledge and understanding of the guidance and legislation that underpins good autism practice.

Thinking point

Why do you think it is important for front line staff to know about the guidance and legislation that has an impact upon their working?

Activity

Have a look at what the National Autistic Society website can tell you about the guidance and legislation that underpins good autism practice in your part of the UK. Talk about this with a colleague, or a person you support, if this is appropriate, or a family carer. Would other people find this information useful? Pass on the details about the National Autistic Society to them.

Key points from this chapter

- It is important to know about the autism strategy for the country that you work in and what it means for the people you support.

- The Human Rights Act is based on the FREDA values of fairness, respect, equality, dignity and autonomy.

- It is important for support workers and people with autistic spectrum conditions and their family carers to know about human rights.

- The Equality Act 2010 replaces the earlier legislation on disability discrimination.

- It is important to remember that laws on capacity assume that all adults are presumed to have capacity to make decisions.

References and where to go for more information

References

Barcham, L and Pountney, J (2011) *Handling Information for Learning Disability Workers.* Exeter: Learning Matters/BILD

Blunden, R (2006) Developing a Welsh Autism Research Centre. *Good Autism Practice Journal*, Volume 7

Centre for Public Scrutiny (2011) *Difference in Mind.* London: National Autistic Society

Fulton, R and Richardson, K (2011) *Equality and Inclusion for Learning Disability Workers.* Exeter: Learning Matters/BILD

Social Care Institute for Excellence (2011) *Improving access to Social Care for adults with autism. SCIE Guide 43.* London: SCIE

Legislation, policies and reports

All UK legislation can be downloaded from www.legislation.gov.uk

Policies and reports for Northern Ireland, Scotland and Wales can be found at www.northernireland.gov.uk, www.scotland.gov.uk and www.wales.gov.uk respectively. Policies and reports for England can be found on the website of the relevant government department.

Department of Health (2009) *The Autism Act* (England) Norwich: TSO

Department of Health (2010) *Fulfilling and Rewarding Lives – The Strategy for Adults with Autism in England.* Norwich: TSO

Northern Ireland Assembly (2011) *Autism Act (Northern Ireland).* Norwich: TSO

The Scottish APS Group (2011) *The Scottish Strategy for Autism.* Edinburgh: The Scottish Government

The Welsh Assembly Government (2008) *The ASD Strategic Action Plan for Wales.* Cardiff: Welsh Government

Adult Support and Protection (Scotland) Act 2007

Adults with Incapacity (Scotland) Act 2000

Equality Act 2010

Human Rights Act 1998

Mental Capacity Act 2005

Protection of Vulnerable Groups (Scotland) Act 2007

Safeguarding Vulnerable Groups Act (2006) (England)

Safeguarding Vulnerable Groups Act 2006 (Controlled Activity) (Wales) Regulations 2010

Websites

A network of regional autism charities www.autism-alliance.org.uk

An online bilingual autism information resource for Wales developed and maintained by Autism Cymru www.awares.org

Autism awareness charity in Scotland www.scottishautism.org

Autism charity for Northern Ireland www.autismni.org

British Institute of Human Rights www.bihr.org.uk

Equality and Human Rights Commission www.equalityhumanrights.com

National Autistic Society (works across the whole of the UK) www.autism.org.uk

Wales national charity for autism www.autismcymru.org

If a clear visual plan is made for an activity, showing the individual what they need to do, and what is going to happen, you will usually find things go much better. This is my experience in my job working with people with autism and severe learning difficulties. It is also true for me in my life. I like to see what is happening and have things written down. It helps me to then know what is happening and decreases anxiety. It also makes things more predictable and everyone needs to remember how much people with autism want and need predictability.

I worry about losing part of any spoken instruction in my head and then not being able to carry out what has been asked. My increased anxiety makes it harder to understand what has been said.

John

Introduction

Understanding the communication differences and difficulties that someone with autism might experience will make a huge difference to your ability to support them well. Having a good understanding of autism means that from the very first time you meet somebody with an autistic spectrum condition, you can communicate effectively, avoiding any communication that might present a difficulty.

In this chapter you will explore why people with autistic spectrum conditions may express emotions that arise from communication difficulties as behaviour that is seen as challenging. You will then learn about the different methods and systems that can be used to help a person develop their communication skills. Finally, the chapter focuses on how you can become an effective communicator with a person with autism.

Learning outcomes

This chapter will help you to:

- explain why behaviour that is seen as challenging can be a way of expressing emotions that occur from communication differences and difficulties;

- describe different methods and systems used to develop and support an individual's communication;

- explain how to maximise the effectiveness of your communication by making verbal and non verbal changes to your communication.

This chapter covers:

Level 3 LD 301 – Understand how to support individuals with autistic spectrum conditions: Learning Outcome 5

Why behaviour that is seen as challenging can be a way of expressing emotions that occur because of communication difficulties

To illustrate this section I want to give an example of someone with an autistic spectrum condition who was in a state of extreme distress and high anxiety. He learnt to enjoy life once more because of the understanding and dedication of the staff team supporting him.

Paul

Paul lives in a residential care home along with six other people who mostly have a diagnosis of autism and a learning disability. There have been a lot of changes recently with the arrival of new staff and also the building being refurbished. These changes and the increased uncertainty they have brought to Paul's life have led to him becoming more reclusive. Paul is communicating his distress by spending longer in his room, refusing to come out, refusing to wear clothes and clearing all of the things out of his room. The manager and support workers are trying really hard with Paul because they care about him a great deal. However, they have a poor understanding of autistic spectrum conditions. They were using their own resources to encourage and persuade Paul out of his room, but the result of all their efforts was a deterioration and further challenging behaviours appearing. Paul started to refuse most meals and only eat a limited range of foods. He began to urinate and defecate in his room and was intolerant of the staff going in and out. On occasions he was violent towards them.

Paul has a limited use of verbal language and when he does speak it is mostly to talk about Postman Pat. He got rid of most of the things from his room, but sometimes he went outside onto the landing just to find a Postman Pat DVD and look at the cover.

Professionals from the local area were called in to support the staff to try and change the way Paul was behaving. They talked to Paul and offered him options. They talked to the staff and listened to their concerns and difficulties. But was anyone really listening to what Paul was communicating? Although he was not using much language, he was speaking loudly and clearly through his behaviour. Without an understanding of autistic spectrum conditions it was impossible to *hear* what Paul was communicating.

Let's analyse the situation using an 'autism aware' approach. Paul was anxious and distressed. He made this very clear by refusing to go out of his room and becoming intolerant of wearing his clothes. This was the point where people needed to hear his distress and to search for the causes. However, as this did not happen in an *'autism friendly'* and *'Paul friendly'* way from the beginning, Paul began to shout louder through his behaviour. Paul was communicating and the priority for those supporting him was to interpret his communication.

Fortunately, the staff team who support Paul were willing to listen and keen to understand autism better so that they could support Paul more effectively. At a special meeting, all of the staff team tried to think with their 'autism hats' on. They first built up a picture of exactly why Paul had become so distressed:

1. The number of new staff members was an issue. Alongside this was the fact that the staff board, with photos of who is on shift and who will be on shift, was no longer accurate. The visual communication of who was going to be on shift was therefore unreliable for Paul. He was anxious because he didn't know which support workers were coming in.

2. The refurbishment of the building was another problem. The main issue for Paul was the fact that the vehicle he loved to travel in was no longer parked outside his window because of the construction work. Due to his autistic spectrum condition Paul cannot think flexibly enough to work out that the vehicle had been parked out of the way nearby. Paul simply didn't know why or where the vehicle had gone.

3. Predictability is very important for people with autistic spectrum conditions. Paul, in his distress, had created a lot of negative predictability to try and calm himself. He had done this through not using the toilet, by clearing his room and not wearing clothes, not eating and at times being aggressive towards staff to ensure that they kept away.

With a clearer understanding of what was being 'said' by Paul, staff were then able to tackle the issues in an autism friendly way. Together the manager and the staff team came up with an action plan that included the following:

1. Stop all of the bubbly and cajoling language. Go into Paul's room in the morning with some breakfast he likes to eat in one hand and a picture of Postman Pat in the other. Don't speak but respond in a simple way if Paul speaks – he may well speak about the Postman Pat picture. Leave Paul alone again. Slowly, over time, build up the communication and the time spent in the room, using the Postman Pat pictures.

2. Update the staff photos on the board and use them consistently and accurately. Involve Paul in the process by showing him the photos of who will be on shift and getting him to put them on the board each day.

3. Park the vehicle in sight of Paul's window once more. Using this as a starting point, encourage Paul to go out again.

This is a simplified and shortened summary of the plan. The whole process of staff thinking about the issues and implementing autism friendly solutions took well over a year. However, the results have been extraordinary. Paul is now dressed for most of the day. He comes out of his room for part of the day and interacts with staff and the other people who live in the home. He goes out in the vehicle every day and will watch his Postman Pat DVDs regularly. He is eating a wider range of food and although staff changes still happen, using the accurate photo board means that Paul knows who will be coming in and out and feels safe. Paul will now point to things and has started to use more language to communicate.

Phoebe Caldwell (2002) wrote a book and produced a DVD entitled *Learning the Language* and this is exactly what the staff supporting Paul have done – but they could not have done it without a good understanding of autism. Through thinking in an 'autistic spectrum conditions way' they were able to hear, interpret and understand Paul's communication.

The story of Paul is a perfect example of challenging behaviour being an attempt to express emotions. Paul was trying to tell staff about things that were greatly distressing him. He wasn't just being difficult or horrible.

There is a danger that we just associate behavioural ways of communicating with those who have limited or no language. Behavioural communication can be equally true for those individuals with autistic spectrum conditions who have a good level of language.

Liam

Liam, a young man with autistic spectrum conditions who is very able and achieving well academically, was found to be the instigator of a sudden spate of blocked toilets and regular floods at his school. He seemed completely unable to explain why he had been doing this and was suspended for three days. At home, even with only limited access to his Xbox, Liam was calm. This situation was a cause of real concern for his family as Liam had been doing well at school and was expected to achieve good grades in his forthcoming 'A' levels. It took his Mum a little while to work out what was happening. Eventually she realised that there had been an increase in talk about the future from various teachers at school, who had started to tell Liam that as he was so bright he would be able to go to the university of his choice. Teachers were using phrases such as the 'world would be his oyster'. These comments had led to an increased sense of anxiety for Liam. He did not want to have to make any choices and he did not like oysters. His way of dealing with the anxiety was to cause some predictable chaos at school. In fact, he had used this coping mechanism in the past, but not been caught. He started to block the toilets, causing a flood. Liam enjoyed the pattern of frustration on the part of the teachers and the caretaker as the problem was sorted each day.

John says, thinking about the effects of choice for him:

One of the areas in life that caused me the most anxiety is that of choice. Both mental health and learning disability professionals are taught in their training to offer those they care for as much choice as possible. This presents a problem for many individuals on the spectrum for whom too much choice can be overwhelming. A few years ago I was helping my brother choose a university by accompanying him across the country to open days. After visiting all five he asked me which I would choose if I were in his position. I thought for a while and said, 'Manchester'. When asked why, I said, 'Because it has the best buses and trains, more radio stations than any other city, and Manchester United play there.' Wisely, he ignored my advice and went to Sheffield. He chose Sheffield because it offered the best course and he liked the accommodation. Manchester appealed to me because it offered predictability and my special interests, I wasn't thinking about my brother's degree or comfort. Often my reaction to a day with too much choice or too many unpredictable things is to go back to bed. It does not occur to me that if I spoke to my family or those I was going to be with that day I could alter the problems and actually take part in something I enjoy. I don't naturally realise that I have the ability to communicate and have an impact on my day. I just get overwhelmed and choose what is the most predictable and needs no talking – bed.

John's words make me think about the many discussions I have had with staff concerning individuals with autism who are very able in many ways, but who appear to be disinterested and even depressed. The staff tell me they *choose* to stay in their room and not join in activities. If we think carefully about the communicative function of their behaviour it may be what is really being said is, 'I can't cope with the choices on offer and the unpredictability.' When we communicate with people with autistic spectrum conditions we need to always remember that they will always have some communication difficulties. We must take account of this when we interpret their behaviour and what they say, and ensure that our own communication is 'autism friendly'.

Thinking point

Do we stop and analyse what an individual's behaviour may be saying, or do we just respond to that behaviour because we are frustrated or confused by it?

Activity

If you work with someone with autism whose behaviour is described as 'challenging' take some time to look at the last few incident report forms that have been completed following an incident. Now consider the behaviour in the light of what we have been looking at in this chapter. What could the behaviour be trying to express? Was the response to that behaviour one that showed a lack of understanding? Discuss this with a colleague or with the individual themselves if this is appropriate.

Different methods and systems used to develop and support an individual's communication

Let's remind ourselves of the key communication difficulties and differences that individuals with autism have, which can lead to behavioural issues. These include delays in processing spoken communication, difficulties in understanding non verbal communication and taking communications literally.

Processing delays

John says:

It may take an individual on the spectrum several minutes or even hours to properly process a piece of communication. This means that the reactions observed by those caring for them are often wrongly interpreted. With me, in the family therapy sessions I attended some time ago, this often meant I was seen as aloof because a seemingly important statement that was made by my parents or the therapist at the time got no reaction from me. Later in the day the statement would cause me great anxiety once I had been able to process what had been said – by then we were somewhere else and I was just left with the anxiety and no ability to deal with it.

Family members and support workers often report how an individual will suddenly give a reply to a question that was asked half an hour ago. This can lead to all sorts of problems. A person with autism may get extremely upset about the fact that the minibus has gone to the swimming session without them, because they have only just said yes. Although they wanted to go swimming they had not understood the conversation at breakfast about the time to go being changed from the afternoon to the morning. Processing delays can be very frustrating for everyone concerned.

Understanding non verbal language

We all communicate non verbally with gestures, posture, facial expressions and our eyes. If none of this is noticed or understood by the individual with autism, it is not surprising that this leads to confusion. The shrug of our shoulders may indicate that we don't know something. However, it may mean nothing to the person with autism who has asked when their key worker is next on shift. If that shrug is accompanied with a comment such as 'heaven knows', the person with autism is left even more confused and anxious. We need to think carefully about what we say with our bodies, eyes, gestures and posture when we are with people with autism.

Taking language very literally

This is an area of communication that often causes laughter in training sessions. Once again, it can be the cause of total miscommunication and can cause a great deal of anxiety for people with autistic spectrum conditions.

Rachel

Rachel is a woman with autism who is very verbal. A new member of staff called Nelson starts supporting Rachel in her home. The first session goes brilliantly and Rachel seems to like Nelson. He gets to know all of Rachel's routines. The next day Nelson calls Rachel 'Miss Buzzy Bee' whilst supporting her to do the recycling. His words are followed by an episode of challenging behaviour and Rachel's insistence that she will have nothing to do with him. It takes time to find out what had gone wrong. Luckily another member of staff has good autism awareness knowledge, and she knows Rachel well. This member of staff uses 'autistic spectrum conditions detective skills' to work out what has gone wrong. She hears Nelson using terms like 'deary' and 'sir' and 'Mr Tidy T' to other people, mainly because he wasn't sure of people's names. When asked what he called Rachel, Nelson remembered he had used the term 'Miss Buzzy Bee'. The other member of staff explained that this was the problem as Rachel does not like bees and she likes to be called by her proper name. Rachel had never heard this term before and only identified with the word 'bee'. Confused and frightened by the mention of something she really didn't like, she had hit out at Nelson. She eventually told the staff member who was a good autistic spectrum conditions detective, 'My name is Rachel and I am not a bee!'

We need to take care over the words we use and the meaning they may give. If we remember this, it will be no surprise that an incident occurs after a member of staff tells a person they support, 'I'll be back in a minute', and half an hour later they are still on the phone.

Thinking point

Do you really say what you mean, and mean what you say, when you talk to the individuals with autistic spectrum conditions whom you work with?

Activity

Observe carefully the interactions that one of your colleagues has with a person with autism, looking particularly at their use of non verbal language. Make a note of the things that you now think may appear confusing and share them with your colleague. You might like to suggest they do the same for you, as it is often very hard to see the confusion your verbal and non verbal communication may be causing.

Visual support

Good visual support is vital for almost all people with autism. The problem is that so many mistakes are made with visual supports. Unfortunately, badly implemented and badly used visual support can be far more damaging than using none at all.

Staff photo boards are a very popular type of visual support. You may well have one in your own workplace. But are they there to explain who works in a particular place or who is working that day? How can we ensure they are kept up to date and accurate? What if a staff member changes their hair colour or shaves off their beard – can we ensure the picture is changed immediately? Even something as basic as a staff photo board needs careful thought and good planning. Even more importantly, it needs a designated person responsible for keeping it up to date and accurate. Easy access to digital photography has made this kind of support much more manageable, but still all too often staff photo boards are neglected or badly used. When this happens it can cause immense fear and anxiety for the people with autism using the service.

Photos of food and meals often cause problems. It is so difficult to ensure that the visual supports make sense to the person and are confirmed by their experience. A photo collection of meals in one home included some photos from the local Chinese takeaway. On one occasion, when people ordered Chinese takeaway, the photo of a particular Chinese meal was up on the board, but one of the people refused his meal when it arrived, clearly due to his high anxiety. It took the staff time to work out what was wrong. They eventually realised that the photo had some prawn crackers on the plate as well as a sweet and sour chicken dish. The meal the person had on that day did not have any prawn crackers and so to them it looked like a very different meal.

Visual support is vital for almost all people with autism – accuracy is important.

TEACCH

The value of accurate visual support must not be underestimated. The work of the TEACCH (**T**reatment and **E**ducation of **A**utistic and related **C**ommunication-handicapped **Ch**ildren) programme, developed in the 1970s in North Carolina, sets out the key principles, and has been copied and followed all over the world. This educational framework, recommended by the National Autistic Society in this country, is based on providing structure to the environment and to the day, with clear visual supports.

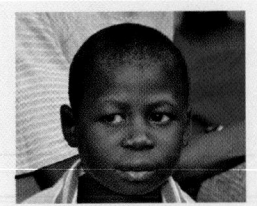

Eric's planner for Tuesday mornings	
Activity	**Notes**
Registration	Go to your form room and read your planner to check your day.
English	Room 114. Take your English book and your pencil case with you.
Break	Choice time in the Autism Base.
Maths	Room 216. Take your maths book, pencil case and maths equipment box.
Geography	Room 224. Take your geography book and pencil case.
Lunch	Today you go to lunch at 12.10. This is the first sitting. After lunch go to the Autism Base and collect your planner for Tuesday afternoon. Read it through.

The example above shows how this kind of support might look. It is worth reading more about this method of working and if possible attending some TEACCH training. With training and knowledge you will be able to accurately implement this kind of structured approach with the right kind of visual supports that will benefit the people that you support. A great resource is *Visual Supports for People with Autism* by Marlene Cohen and Donna Sloan (you can find further details on this book at the end of this chapter).

PECS

The Picture Exchange Communication System (PECS), devised by Andy Bondy and Lori Frost in 1998, is now widely used as a way of teaching functional communication to children with autism. It is especially suitable for children who are non verbal or who have little language. Each child is assessed to find the objects or activities that they find rewarding. They are then taught to make spontaneous requests for these items. One adult is identified as the *communication partner* and a second adult as the *physical prompter*. The latter's task is to guide the child to pick up a picture of the object to give to their communication partner, who then ensures that they receive what has been requested. This forms the basis of further developments, with spontaneous communication being the aim.

There is some good evidence based research that shows the value of the PECS system for children with autism who have little or no language (Howlin et al, 2007). The difficulty is that in some services that support people with autism, they say in their promotional literature that they are using PECS, when in fact only basic visual supports are being used. They may have no idea what PECS stands for, what the communication system is or how it is supposed to work. PECS is often stated as being used when services want to appear more autism specific. Claims like this dilute the value of the PECS system and create confusion.

I think it is far better that we are clear about the value of visual supports and that we work on getting a few of them correct and consistent, than to make claims about the implementation of a specific communication system. It is great if there is the opportunity for good family and staff training about the communication system being used, to ensure consistency. But where this is not possible, it is important to tell the truth to individuals with autism in the way that we use pictures and photos as a support.

There is very real value in simple, clear, and accurate visual supports. Cards that just show what we are going to do first, and then that we will do something the individual wants to do next, are of tremendous value. Similarly, an accurate diary or calendar that shows when mum or dad is coming to visit for example, can give the person you support a reliable and consistent predictability which makes them feel safe and happy.

First   **Then**

Thinking point

When did you last make use of a digital camera? Do you know where the digital camera is at work and how to access it? Do you know how to upload the photos and print them off?

Activity

If you don't know where to find the digital camera at your workplace, try to find out. Learn not only how to use the camera, but how to ensure you can get the photos needed to support your communication with those you work with. Keep it very simple and always remember to update regularly any photographic support you put in place.

Ways to maximise the effectiveness of our own communication

In this chapter we have thought about the key areas of difficulty for good communication with people with autistic spectrum conditions. These include:

- processing delay;

- lack of understanding of non verbal language;

- literal interpretation of spoken language.

We have also touched on some of the specific interventions that will support effective communication. Both TEACCH and PECS require significant staff training in order to be understood and to work properly. However, making use of visual supports more generally, and keeping them up to date and relevant to the person you support, can be of real value and can be done even with minimal staff training. In this final section it is the idea of being more self aware and making use of simple, but clear, support systems that I want to concentrate on. Each of us can make a big difference to the lives of those with autism we work or live with, **IF** we think in a more autism friendly way and, through this, adopt an autism friendly approach.

The processing delay

Give people time! Be prepared to ask a question or give an instruction and then **WAIT**. Try not to repeat yourself unless you are asked to and especially try not to repeat yourself with additional flowery language that you think will make things clearer. This will undoubtedly cause more confusion. Use minimal, clear language and be patient.

I would like to share an example from my own practice. It shows us that even when we know what we should be doing because we have good autism knowledge, we can often still do the wrong thing because neurotypical behaviour comes so naturally to those not on the spectrum.

The cycling trip

I was going cycling in a forest with a colleague and two young men with autistic spectrum conditions, both of whom were quite able and very verbal. The bike hire place was quite busy so I quickly parked the car. One of the young men got out of the front of the car and lifted his seat for my colleague and the other young man to get out of the back. However, the young man in the back did not attempt to get out. After a while I was getting a bit anxious and tried to cajole him out by saying, 'Come on Ben! Or we will be stuck in the queue and I know you are looking forward to the bike ride. Quick, quick, let's get going! No dawdling now! There are lots of people and we will be stuck behind them if you are not snappy.' Ben continued to sit there. It was the other young man who reminded me that, like him, Ben had autism and if I stopped talking to him and just waited a few moments he would be able to get out of the car. He just needed time for the transition and time to process my first request before I had added a string of additional words and noises. So I waited. And after about four minutes Ben got out of the car and we had a great day on the bikes.

We were in real danger of having had a very bad day because I had not been thinking in an autism friendly way. We need to constantly ask ourselves how our own communication is being interpreted, and if it really is autism aware.

We must think before we speak. If we take care to use minimal language and then give the person plenty of time to process and consider what has been said, we are far more likely to get a positive response. Communicating in this way does not come naturally and we have to work at it.

Non verbal language

What can we do about something that is part of who we are and how we communicate instinctively every day? First, be self aware, take notice of the things that you do that convey meaning to others with your eyes, your hands and your facial expressions. If you are more self aware you are more likely to consider your physical actions and movements.

In the past, as a teacher in an ordinary classroom, I would use the whole range of my body language in order to engage the young people. As a teacher of young people with autistic spectrum conditions I learnt to do the opposite. I limited my non verbal language as much as possible and kept my voice as much to a monotone as possible. This style minimises any distraction from the actual words.

The whole of society cannot constantly communicate in an autism friendly way. For the vast majority of people, gesture, body language and a complex and subtle use of language comes entirely naturally and forms part of who they are. Of course, in a professional context, we can adapt our ways of communicating to help the people we support. However, we also need to go one step further, and teach people coping strategies and increase their understanding so that they can function in the neurotypical world. The starting point for this is to help people with autism develop good self awareness themselves, so that they understand that the way they are feeling is because they have autistic spectrum conditions. From that point they can learn how best to deal with the particular issues and go on to live a full and rich life. Even individuals with complex needs and learning disabilities can be helped to have some level of self awareness and understand something of their autism. I have always found this to be hugely beneficial and would encourage you to seek guidance on helping individuals to understand themselves and their autism whenever possible.

Literal interpretation of language

Once again this is about thinking in an autism friendly way and really trying to say exactly what you *mean*. So, for example don't ever say, 'I will be back in a minute,' unless you really mean you will return in 60 seconds or less. It is far better to say something along the lines of 'first' and 'then', for example, 'First, I have to make one phone call and then I will be with you.' Don't just say, 'We will go to the shops later.' Instead, it is far better to be clear about what has to be done first and to give an estimated time of when you will leave to go shopping, for example between 2 and 2.15pm. Always try to be precise, literal and use minimal language.

Jokes and innuendo are the hardest for people with autistic spectrum conditions to grasp and so often cause confusion and anxiety. Take, for example, the member of staff who tells a person they support, 'It will take more than all the tea in China to make me go bowling with you again.'

The individual spoken to loves bowling and knows this member of staff will be supporting them next week when he is scheduled to go bowling again. He does not process all the words being spoken and has no awareness that this is a joke, because he beat the member of staff at a game. We can set someone up to be anxious all week using language in this very neurotypical way. It is, of course, important for individuals with autism to have some understanding of jokes and we can help with this by telling them we are going to make a joke and explaining it. They still might not get the joke, but in my experience, what does happen is that they grasp that people make jokes, so when they next can't understand the meaning of what is said, they may well ask if you are joking. This is a useful skill and can alleviate much anxiety as it gets us to explain ourselves better and to inform people when we are joking or not.

There is a great deal we can do to maximise the effectiveness of our own communication. We can support the communication development of people with autistic spectrum conditions by teaching them about non verbal language and the meanings of words. We can help them to grasp what a joke is. We can encourage them in their use of visual supports, whether it is pictures, lists, calendars, diaries, daily schedules or written instructions. Never underestimate how much time and effort is involved in establishing effective communication supports, but remember what a huge difference you are making to somebody's life through your efforts and perseverance.

I never go to meet someone with autism without a note pad, and I will often have my name and their name written on the first page. I may then write a few key words down as we talk to draw their attention to these words. I may draw a picture to support what is being said. I will show them, in my diary, the day and date we are due to meet again and follow this up with a letter that is clear and concise about what was said in our meeting, what the outcomes were and when we are meeting again.

My three most important tools for effective autism friendly communication are my digital camera (that has a big screen on the back so we can look at the photo instantly), a note pad and a pen. You should have easy access to these resources. We often talk and read about the communication difficulties that people with autistic spectrum conditions have. We must remember that communication is a two way process and that we are the other half of the communication relationship. Therefore, we are also half of the problem. If we can take small steps to adjust and adapt the way we work we will make a massive difference to the lives of the people we support.

Where possible make things visual to aid communication.

Key points from this chapter

- Communication is more than talking.

- When people with autism can talk well remember they still have a communication problem.

- When people with autistic spectrum conditions can't talk they may well understand much more than you realise.

- Be self aware – consider your voice, tone, posture, body language and what you wear.

- Where possible make things visual, to aid communication.

References and where to go for more information

References

Bogdashina, O (2004) *Communication Issues in Autism and Asperger Syndrome.* London: Jessica Kingsley

Caldwell, P (2007) *From Isolation to Intimacy – Making Friends Without Words.* London: Jessica Kingsley

Caldwell, P (2002) *Learning the Language.* Brighton: Pavilion Press

Cohen, M J and Sloan, D L (2008) *Visual Supports for People with Autism.* Bethesda, MD: Woodbine House Publishers

Howlin, P et al (2007) The effectiveness of the Picture Exchange Communication System (PECS) training for teachers of children with autism: a pragmatic group randomised trial. *Journal of Child Psychology and Psychiatry,* Volume 48, no. 5, pp. 473–81

Welton, J (2004) *Say What You Mean and Mean What You Say.* London: Jessica Kingsley

Chapter 6

Understanding how to support individuals with autistic spectrum conditions

Conner was collected by his mum every other weekend for his home visit. I noticed when she came to collect Conner that she stood and waited quietly. Conner would go up to her, bury his head in her neck and take a deep sniff, then his head came up beaming and he and his mum hugged each other. He needed to check it was his mum by smelling her! This may be quite extreme but often when I am working with staff teams the problem of someone who wants to sniff staff members is an issue that gets discussed. The idea that this is how they really know who you are is thought to be surprising, but in following up the stories raised it is often found to be true. The challenge is to have a more acceptable way of allowing an individual to use their sense of smell to know who is working with them on that day. One simple thing that can be done is to stick to the same perfume or aftershave to try and ensure that you do always smell the same. It may sound odd but it is all part of maintaining predictability on a sensory level.

Sue Hatton, talking about person centred support

Introduction

In this chapter we will explore ideas that will enable us to offer better support to individuals with autistic spectrum conditions and their families. As we have tried to make clear throughout the book, the secret lies in a better understanding of the nature of autism and how it affects each person that we are working with. Everyone with an autistic spectrum condition is different. Whenever we meet someone new, we need to begin that exploration of the autistic spectrum again and consider its impact on that specific individual. This is the only way to be truly person centred.

Learning outcomes

This chapter will help you to:

- explain the importance of being person centred and aware of each individual's preferences and needs;

- explain why consultation with the family and other carers is important when providing person centred support;

- describe different techniques and approaches to support individuals with autistic spectrum conditions in their learning and development;

- explain how to reduce sensory overload or increase sensory stimulation by adapting the physical and sensory environment;

- outline ways to support an individual to protect themselves from harm;

- explain how needs change for individuals and families at different stages in life;

- describe the role that advocacy can play in the support of people with autistic spectrum conditions.

This chapter covers:

Level 3 LD 301 – Understand how to support individuals with autistic spectrum conditions: Learning Outcome 6

The importance of being person centred and aware of each individual's preferences and needs

To illustrate the nature of being person centred in an 'autism aware' and 'autism friendly' way I am going to share two stories. The first is about John and myself going to do some training together. This is something we have done many times in different parts of the country. However, the difficulties experienced on this occasion indicate how important it is to keep thinking in autism friendly ways – even when you think you know someone well. The second story is about Elizabeth and her son Edward. Elizabeth obviously knows her son extremely well, but her story gives us another example of how you always have to keep the autism of the individual in mind. It is important not to become complacent or slip into making assumptions about what might or might not happen. If we are seeking to work in an autism friendly way, we will be planning and preparing the support we offer all the time.

Story 1: A training session in Scotland

John and I were asked to carry out two days' training in the north east of Scotland. It was a long journey involving a flight and car hire. John likes planes and using public transport; with buses being one of his special interests. He enjoys earning the money that comes from giving talks and John and I get on well. I had planned for us to stay in a nice hotel with some good food and it did not occur to me that there might be any difficulties for John. I had become complacent and was not thinking about the nature of John's autism and the things that are so important for him. I know about his special interests and how much pleasure and calmness they bring to him, but I did not think about the impact of the lack of access to them for the two days we were away. Neither did John, as he tends to live very much in the moment, like many people with autism.

During the two days, John coped with the familiar and predictable pattern of training and the kinds of questions that people ask as they are so often the same. However, at times he really struggled and was unhappy and quite distressed during the trip. This resulted in him spending as much time as he could asleep and shut off from the world.

John shared his feelings with me:

> I don't understand how people can live in a place as remote as this. We have been here two days and seen only 10 buses in the whole of that time. There is no train station and hardly any local radio. I was a bit worried before we came

about these things but I did not realise how awful it could be in the countryside when it is winter and dark and the weather is not very good. I should have bought some bus timetables with me to look at, enjoy, and spend time with.

I was surprised by how awful John found the experience. I wrongly thought that he would enjoy the time with me, the food, staying in a hotel – how neurotypical of me – it was as if I had left my 'autism lens' behind. None of the things that I have referred to mean much to John. In fact, during our debrief about the whole experience, John shared with me that he actually finds it hard work eating a meal with others. He wants and needs to concentrate on one thing. Eating his food whilst social chit chat goes on around him can be quite distressing, and, although he has learnt to be able to cope, he would actually prefer to eat on his own.

What should I have done? I should have planned the whole venture in a much more autism friendly way. This should have involved preparing with John for the experience of a very rural setting and putting in place support to enable him to cope with the challenges. John rightly suggested taking bus timetables. One of John's other loves is politics. As we were in Scotland it would have been helpful to have found some literature regarding Scottish politics for him to read and for us to discuss. It would also have been helpful if John had been able to think through the difficulties he may have experienced prior to going. For the two of us, it was a steep learning curve and an experience from which we have learnt a great deal.

Story 2: Elizabeth and Edward

Elizabeth's experience with Edward was very similar, although Edward has what is often described as classic autism and is non verbal. Edward loves Disneyland and the family were going again to Euro Disney. They were confident of his enjoyment and, of course, know their son very well. However, complacency had set in and they did not take the usual visual supports that they used to help Edward understand what was happening. Why bother? He had been many times and always loved it!

This time there was a key difference as it was extremely hot. Edward found the temperature hard to cope with and his ability to know that if they walked across the concrete boulevard they would arrive at his favourite café for a drink and ice-cream was beyond him. Elizabeth and her husband really wished they had brought the pictures to remind Edward of what would come after the short walk, but they had not. The more they spoke and cajoled, the harder Edward found the heat and in the end he gave up and sat in the middle of a large concrete boulevard on the floor and refused to move. The visual support of a picture of an ice-cream would have been so valuable at this point but neither Elizabeth nor her husband had one with them.

Edward sat on the floor and seemed to shut down. Elizabeth cried and her husband had an idea and went and obtained a wheelchair. This worked and they were finally able to get Edward to move. The wheelchair remained a part of this holiday.

Almost as soon as they arrived home they began preparations for the next holiday. Elizabeth knew they had got things wrong by not thinking in an autism friendly way ALL of the time for Edward. They had made the assumption that, as he had been many times before, all would be well. They had not considered visiting Euro Disney in a heat wave and that, because of his autism, Edward wasn't able to transfer his experiences easily. The next holiday in Italy was a great success, mainly because they went well prepared with every visual support that could have been required. Edward knew for the whole of the holiday what was happening NOW and what was going to happen NEXT – and they made sure NEXT was always a real motivator for Edward. For this family, it was the recipe for an enjoyable and autism friendly holiday.

The two stories above illustrate this point well but let's look at an example from the setting of a residential care home where several people with autistic spectrum conditions live.

The importance of visual support to aid communication is a common thread running through this book. One common tool seen in many homes is a staff photo board to show who is working that day or shift. If done properly and kept up to date, this can often bring calmness and security to an individual getting up in a morning who may be anxious about who will be on shift that day. However, sometimes this does not work very well. In one service I worked in, we ended up taking the board down as one particular resident had a favourite member of staff whom they wanted to see every day. If her photo was on the board he would be happy and if it was not he would become very stressed and take down other staff photos and destroy them, hoping that this might mean her picture would go up. In the end we took the whole board down.

However, this was not really fair on the other people living in the home who benefitted from the board. To solve this, staff photo boards were created and maintained in each of their rooms. This created more work, but was a person centred approach, that took into account each individual's preferences and needs. For the one resident who wanted the same person every day, a different approach was required. Staff started to work on helping this individual understand what the staff member was doing when she wasn't at work. In addition, they started trying to ensure that the individual enjoyed working with different staff members so that he could be happy and calm with a wider range of people. Initially, this was a lot more work for everyone involved, however, if support can be person centred from the start, we will find the need for less work in the long run. Creating staff photo boards in every room meant extra work including making sure there were eight copies of every staff member's photo, one for each of the eight residents, and also ensuring that there were spares. This also meant changing the photos if someone had their hair cut short or when new staff started. This led to happy and calm mornings in a home where eight people lived together – the benefits far outweigh this investment of time and energy.

We must remember that a person centred plan is much more than getting a staff photo board in the right place at the right time. *Valuing People* (2001) and *Valuing People Now* (2009), government policies relating to support for people with a learning disability in England, had a positive influence on all health and social care organisations, making them more person centred. More recently, *Fulfilling and Rewarding Lives* (2010), the strategy for adults with autism in England, has highlighted the need to understand autism in order to be able to offer person centred support.

To produce a good person centred plan for someone with an autistic spectrum condition requires a good understanding of the nature of autism and how it impacts upon each individual. Only then can progress be made. If this level of autism awareness is not in place then the danger is that people will not make progress or will take some steps and then complacency will set in to the support structures and the individual concerned will deteriorate.

You can find out more about person centred planning and person centred support in the book by Liz Tilly in this series, *Person Centred Approaches when Supporting People with a Learning Disability* (2011).

Thinking point

Think about the ways you are currently providing good person centred support. Reflect on whether this meets the needs and aspirations of the person you support.

Activity

Visual supports are often created and then get forgotten or are allowed to deteriorate. Consider your place of work and the people you support. Have a look at the person centred plan for someone you support with autistic spectrum conditions. Are there some visual supports referred to as part of that plan? Do they need renewing or replacing? If so, get this done the next time that you are in work and add something to the plan about the importance of maintaining this kind of support structure. Don't let complacency set in. A person centred plan needs to be a living document. Is this the case for the people you support?

The importance of consultation with the family and other carers when providing person centred support

It is quite common for me to hear staff in services complaining about a parent or the family of someone they support in the following way:

They are nice people and they love their son. But they need to understand that he is an adult now even though he does have autism. They tend to mollycoddle him and spoil him when he goes home for a weekend and it just causes so much difficulty for us when he comes back.

Or

> They make such a fuss and are always on the phone checking things with us. They need to learn to let her go now, they fuss about what she wears and how her hair is. They need to learn to leave these things to us now.

Let us look at this from the perspective of a parent, as we hear a mum called Jane speak about her experiences with her son.

Jane says:

The staff are nice enough but he is MY son and it was so hard to let him leave home. We want the best for him, like for all our children and I get upset if I go to collect him and he is looking scruffy and his hair has not been combed properly. Also, when they send him home for a weekend things get forgotten like his pyjamas. One weekend they even sent him home with a t-shirt that was not his. If they can't get his clothes right, how can I be sure they are getting his care and support right? It is such a worry and when I phone I feel a nuisance as they are busy and don't seem to have time to talk. However, if he gets upset and there is some kind of an incident they are on the phone quick enough to tell me about it. It is not easy letting your vulnerable adult son be cared for by other people. I wish they would understand that.

Getting to know the family of a person you support is a good way of getting to know the individual better.

Another parent of a young man with autism and learning disabilities has some very good advice that she gives when training and talking about the importance of the relationship between parents and carers. She talks of the importance of being able to share something of the 'journey' she has been on as a parent of a child with autism. She also emphasises that there is a need for those who are now caring for him to hear her story and realise that it is a journey that she and her son are still on. As staff, they may join them for a short period, but she is on this journey for her lifetime. She says how good it is to get a phone call that is about something positive and not just to be called when there is a problem. She says she starts to dread the sound of the manager's or key worker's voice. A phone call from such people should be positive and constructive.

What can be difficult for anyone with autistic spectrum conditions, staff and family members, is to try and step into each other's shoes, yet this can be so beneficial. This can bring a very different perspective. I know that when Elizabeth, who has helped in the writing of this book, was challenged to go and shadow some shifts in a care home, her attitude towards those who cared for her son altered. She realised the challenges that support workers faced when getting eight people up, dressed and ready for the day. In the same way, when staff have sat and listened to a parent tell their story, a big shift in attitude takes place. We need to listen carefully to each other and not make assumptions about why things are said or done.

John has something to share with us about involving his parents:

> Once I became 18, there were professionals who felt it was right and proper to keep my meetings about me and the support I needed. They didn't encourage my parents to be involved in the same way they had in the past. This was upsetting and frightening for me. I wanted and still want, even though I am now 24, my parents to be very involved. I need their guidance and support and I trust them.

Carole, John's mum, says:

> When John first got his diagnosis it was very hard for me and I felt as if in some ways I was to blame. Being asked questions like, 'Was John planned?' upset me a great deal. Now he is an adult, I feel we sometimes have to really push to be part of discussions about support for John and yet we know he wants us involved. I don't know why it is so hard for professionals and family members to work well together, we should be able to as we both want the best for the person concerned. It is about listening, and as a parent I don't get listened to enough.

The most person centred and effective way to support the individuals with autistic spectrum conditions you work with is to try and get to know the families as well as you know their son or daughter. Try sharing the good experiences and activities that go on at least five times more than the problems. A phone call out of the blue to tell a parent that their son or daughter has achieved something means so much. Getting to know the family is a very good way of getting to know the individual and enabling you as a member of staff to work in a more person centred way.

Thinking point

Do you know what the best family holiday experience was for each person that you support?

Activity

If you don't know about the best family holiday experience try and find out. There might be some photos that you could copy and have in a folder for the individuals to look at or for staff to share with them. Photos are a great way of sharing an experience and are very autism friendly.

Elizabeth and her son Edward with the rest of the family on an adventurous holiday in Austria.

Different techniques and approaches to support individuals with autistic spectrum conditions to learn and develop their skills

There are a considerable number of specific approaches that have been developed in working with people with autistic spectrum conditions. They are often referred to as 'interventions'. It is worth knowing about these so that you can explore them further (they have also been referred to in Chapter 3 in this book). We will then return to look at the general principles for good autism practice as these are really the foundation for effective person centred support.

TEACCH

TEACCH (Treatment and Education of Autistic and related Communication-handicapped Children) is an approach that comes originally from North Carolina. It is about providing structure to the individual's environment and to their day. It works very much on harnessing the visual skills that many people with autistic spectrum conditions have and developing these to help them follow a routine. There is a tendency for this and other approaches to get watered down, misunderstood or applied in an unhelpful fashion. The TEACCH approach, with its emphasis on structure and the use of visual support, is very much the foundation of many other approaches and is central to good autism practice. The one drawback that is sometimes raised is that some people can become too dependent on the prompts of the visual supports and are not able to cope without them. A gradual reduction of lots of prompts and an ability to put them back in again if the individual's anxiety increases is a good approach. This TEACCH approach was designed by Eric Schopler and Gary Mezibov and one of their books is listed in the references section at the end of this chapter.

The Lovaas Approach

This is an intervention developed by Ivar Lovaas (1987) and colleagues from the University of California. It is a behavioural approach with the focus on getting the child to understand that every behaviour has a consequence, undesirable behaviours are modified and more desirable behaviours are acquired. The aim is that the desirable behaviour is reinforced with a reward and the undesirable is ignored, which will then lead to the eradication of undesirable behaviour. There has been considerable controversy over this approach, but many families still seek what has been claimed to be a method of recovery from autism. The programme is very intensive with on average 40 hours a week of one to one work with the child.

The Son-Rise or Options Approach

Like the Lovaas approach, this is an intervention that has claimed that 'recovery from autism' is possible and it is therefore controversial. However, there are significant differences as it is very child centred and is based on following the child's lead and their interests. These interests are then used to begin interaction and join in with what the child is focused on. There is a real focus on accepting what the child finds significant and seeing the parent as the most important teacher for their son or daughter. This includes elements of an approach known as intensive interaction, which is also very person focused and based on valuing each person's interests, no matter how unusual. Intensive interaction is an approach that is used much more with adults; the focus of the Lovaas and Son-Rise approaches is with young children. You can find out where to access further information about these approaches in the references section at the end of this chapter.

There are many more alternative approaches and you should find out more about the ones that are relevant to the needs of the people you work with. Each approach has something to contribute and some will have more to offer than others for each individual. This includes the Higashi or Daily Life Therapy that came to the UK from Japan via Boston. Regular exercise is a key part of this approach.

There are also interventions that have been developed to address particular aspects of autistic spectrum conditions, such as the communication difficulties and differences or the social interaction difficulties – for example, the Picture Exchange Communication System (PECS) and Social Stories as developed by Carol Gray. To find out more about these approaches look at the references section at the end of this chapter.

It is important to have a good understanding of autistic spectrum conditions and the ways it impacts on individuals; this is how you will be better equipped to work in a truly person centred way.

The National Autistic Society developed the helpful acronym, SPELL. This stands for:

S Structure

P Positive – work on building strengths

E Empathy – for the way they see the world

L Low Arousal – to cover the sensory stimulation and also the way people interact with the individual.

L Links – the importance of family links to ensure consistency and predictability in how the individual is supported.

It is a really helpful way of remembering some of the important things when supporting people with autism.

Activity

Find out more about SPELL, the approach developed by the National Autistic Society, then list the five elements that make up the SPELL approach: structure, positive, empathy, low arousal and links. With a colleague, or at your next team meeting, discuss how you can implement each of the five elements in SPELL to support someone to learn new skills.

How to reduce sensory overload or increase sensory stimulation by adapting the physical and sensory environment

John says:
Sensory overload is one of the biggest challenges faced by people with autism. In order to face this effectively, it is vital to understand that sensory issues are often massively exacerbated by anxiety, so it is often wise to consider that, as far as possible, situations that bring anxiety are moderated. This is of course not always possible, and there are times when a visit to a shopping centre is unavoidable or having people round for a meal, but it is always best to define clearly and concisely how long an individual's exposure to these situations will

be. Parents and carers must ensure that they always stick to any commitments regarding time, even though it may be inconvenient to them. This is just as true for me as it is for other people with autistic spectrum conditions. A whole range of things can raise my anxiety levels and this reduces my ability to cope with ordinary situations that other people handle with ease. Unless I am encouraged and enabled to access one of my special interests, my anxiety can become out of control, but a bus journey and a timetable for that bus route to look at will help to put me back on an even keel. I find socialising very stressful, when lots of people are talking at once. I find it anxiety-making when I meet people I know but am not expecting to see them, I don't know what to do or say. I actually find it quite stressful eating with other people as I can't concentrate on the food and what is being said at the same time. I would prefer to eat on my own but I know I need to cope with eating with others. However, this is stressful for me.

One of the most important things to remember about sensory overload is that often it is very difficult to predict what situations will cause anxiety, due to the individual's uneven cognitive profile, and often parents and carers will have to react to situations as they encounter them. One of the first pieces of advice my parents were given after my diagnosis was that they would notice changes in my state of mind long before I was able to, and that they would have to act long before I even realised there was something wrong. One of the strategies that has proved effective for some parents and carers is to have their bag full of 'simple sensory stuff', such as elastic bands or spinning tops, to provide a short term predictable sensory 'anti-stimulation'. For me, (unless I can jump on a bus) it is a piece of yellow card with the word LUNCH written on it. It is covered in Sellotape and I carry this in my pocket. I like to flap it and pass it through my fingers. I find this a calming distraction to other sensory difficulties like lots of people talking.

LUNCH

Thinking point

If you were to start working with John, how might you try to begin your relationship?

Activity

List three ways that John's autism has impacted on his senses, then consider how to successfully support John in relation to sensory issues.

People with autistic spectrum conditions often experience their senses very differently from us and their sensory processing can be quite debilitating. As we explore the way that autism is impacting on an individual this will include an understanding of the way their senses are processing what goes on around them. What is it that they find uncomfortable? What is it from a sensory point of view that they find stimulating and enjoyable? It is good to see the increase of the use of sensory profiling for people with autistic spectrum conditions. An occupational therapist (OT) with good autistic spectrum conditions knowledge is very valuable to any autism service or individual. They are able to produce a sensory profile which will highlight the difficulties and differences and will also be able to suggest a range of activities that can help to reduce painful stimulation caused by certain noises, lighting, or tastes. Don't feel that you have to wait for an OT before you start thinking about someone's sensory issues. Be observant and make some notes in relation to:

● Hearing – What is the person sensitive to? Are there noises they like and enjoy? What can we do to reduce the painful noises and facilitate those that are enjoyed? Ear defenders, ear plugs, listening to their own music are all simple things that can help. It is often sudden, unexpected noises that are particularly painful, like fire alarms or dogs barking. If possible, giving people a warning can be very helpful, so that they can prepare for the noise.

● Vision – What are they sensitive to? Are there things they like to see? Different kinds of lighting can be crucial; up-lighting can be less stressful for people with autistic spectrum conditions. It may be particular colours or patterns can cause problems. When we find out about these, we must make sure that other staff know, for example, that someone will not eat from the blue plates and must have a green one.

● Taste – There are many factors regarding the taste, texture and predictability of food. Some people like it soft and mushy, some like it hard and crunchy. For people with autistic spectrum conditions the experiences are often much more exaggerated and again can cause considerable stress. It is very possible for people to learn to tolerate and even like a wider range of food if their diet is restricted, but this takes time and patience.

- Touch – On the DVD, *A is for Autism*, Temple Grandin talks about touch feeling painful when she was young. She says she found a cuddle from her Mum was like the feeling of being swallowed. Temple Grandin went on to build herself a squeeze machine based on the type that is used to hold cattle still. This is something she was able to control, as she found the pressure calming; unlike the touch of another person that she could not control. Some other people with autistic spectrum conditions love to be touched by people and will seek it out, sometimes inappropriately.

- Smell – There are some people for whom certain smells are totally unbearable, when we might not be able to smell anything at all. Other people recognise others more by their smell than by the sound of their voice or by looking at their face. If you work with someone who recognises others mostly by their smell, then wearing the same deodorant or using the same shampoo when you go to work will help them to recognise you. It will contribute to the predictability in their environment.

Thinking point

Have you ever considered the impact that you personally may have on someone with autistic spectrum conditions if you wear bright clothes or strong perfume? We need to think about a low arousal appearance as well as working in a low arousal way!

Activity

With a colleague, discuss the issues for someone with autism that you work with, in relation to the seven senses, as listed on page 19. Write down what you both notice about each sense for that individual. Is there something new you now think you need to take account of and if so what will you do? You may also need to make sure your colleagues are more aware of their own sensory issues.

Supporting an individual to keep safe from harm

Teaching people with autism to keep themselves safe is extremely important, but also quite hard to achieve. Let's have a look at a few difficulties that have affected individuals with autistic spectrum conditions that I know.

John shares that when walking to and from a football ground his Dad will sometimes tell him that they are going a different way and quickly walks in a new direction, which seems strange to John. What John will not have noticed or have been aware of is any potential trouble between fans ahead; because John has difficulty reading people in a way his father does not. In fact, John says sometimes he can feel drawn towards the odd behaviour of a group of fans, completely unaware of the danger this might put him in.

One man that I know with autism finds watching children playing fascinating, especially if they are playing in water. In the past he has been found standing and staring at the antics of young children in a paddling pool in the park. This has led people to believe that there is something sinister in his attraction to the children. They would be so wrong. It is the splashing of the water and the antics of the children that amuse him and he loves to watch this. In fact, he would not want to interact with any of the children at all, but his behaviour makes people who do not know him think otherwise. Without help and support encouraging him not to stare he is making himself extremely vulnerable to accusations and misunderstanding.

A woman called Pauline takes delight in asking tall men in the supermarket to get items from the top shelf for her. She explains that what she enjoys is the pattern of asking and the men usually saying yes and lifting the item down to put in her basket. She likes it so much that she either seeks out the tall men or follows the first one she asks around the supermarket to keep asking for his assistance. This enjoyment of a simple pattern of behaviour actually makes her very vulnerable in a public place.

So what can we do? We can try and teach people more about understanding the impact of their own behaviour as well as the behaviour of others. This can be hard to do as it focuses on one of the main challenges for people with autism, social interaction. However, we should try even if this results in simply teaching a set of rules. You then have to cope with the consequence of those rules being followed all the time with no room for discretion. An example of how difficult this can be is when people are told, 'Don't talk to strangers'. Talking to strangers is something that we do all the time, when we buy a ticket at the train station, or stamps at the post office. It happens when we respond to someone's comment at the bus stop or apologise for knocking into someone at the supermarket. We can, and should, try to teach some rules, but remember it is not easy for people with autism, for whom everything in life is much more black and white with very little grey.

One very helpful strategy is to teach people with autistic spectrum conditions over a period of time to create a 'hand of trust'. This involves identifying five people from amongst their family, friends or support staff, who can be linked to the four fingers and one thumb on their hand. For example, in Joe's life it works as follows.

Joe's hand of trust

Five people he can check things out with, five people whom he knows he can trust and who will support him to make decisions. Five people who understand Joe's vulnerability and his autism and who will do what they can to support him well.

The thumb represents Mum.

The forefinger is brother Jim.

The tallest finger is support worker Joanne

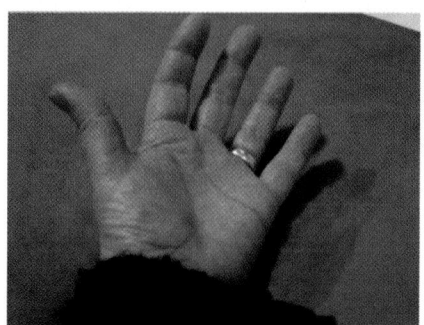

The next finger represents Joe's doctor, whom he has known for years

The little finger stands for Mum's friend Anne

If Joe is approached in the street by someone selling or canvassing he will excuse himself and say he needs to check things out with someone from his hand of trust before he will answer or make a commitment. If he is cold-called on the phone he will be polite and say he needs first of all to check things with one of these five people. This is true even when his advocacy group are planning a day trip to the seaside – Joe will not say he is going until he has talked it through with one person from his hand of trust. It may sound rather cumbersome and even rather restrictive, but for many people with autism it can help to take away their anxiety around their vulnerability. It can even help them to begin to learn how to weigh things up when making a decision like whether to trust someone new or not. It may seem a rather over protective strategy, but it can be quite liberating as well as providing security for a potentially vulnerable individual.

As staff working with individuals with autistic spectrum conditions you will have completed your safeguarding training. It is important to think about that training and consider some of the implications of the training in relation to people with autism. The difficulties they have in understanding how relationships work can make them vulnerable in a variety of ways. This is why the hand of trust idea is so useful.

The book by Simon Bickerton in this series, *Principles of Safeguarding and Protection for Learning Disability Workers* (2011) will help you learn more about safeguarding issues.

How needs change for individuals and families at different stages in life

In some ways this may sound rather obvious as needs change for all families and individuals as time goes on. The need to think about this in an autism friendly way and address problems that change brings for people with autistic spectrum conditions, is vital. Both large and small transitions need to be prepared for and well supported. It may be a tough time for all children making the move to secondary school, but for the child with autism, getting used to a new school is likely to take months rather than days. A good level of preparation and support through the process is needed. This may be followed by quite a settled period, especially if there are aspects of school that the child really enjoys or excels at. Coming up to leaving school can become a very frightening time with choices to be made. What is exciting for some 18 year olds is almost too much to cope with for an 18 year old with autism. Once again, much more support and preparation time is needed for the person with autism and their family at such a time of anxiety. Always remember that choice and decision making can be very stressful rather than exciting for people with autistic spectrum conditions.

It is possible for the move from the family home to living in another environment to go smoothly if planned and thought through properly. Elizabeth speaks about their first visit to Edward's adult placement and how a member of staff opened the door to greet them holding a box of the kind of bricks Edward loved. He was more than happy to go in and sit on the floor with his bricks while an anxious mum and dad looked around. Six years on, Edward is reasonably settled and enjoys a range of activities in his residential care home. For Elizabeth the journey back to the family home after a weekend together remains a tearful one and this is likely to continue for a very long time. Staff need to be aware of this and support her in this 'letting go' each time she visits, and also to reassure her regularly that Edward is settled and content.

Thinking point

What small change have you experienced that had a BIG impact on someone with autistic spectrum conditions you know?

Activity

Think ahead about a change that is going to occur for an individual you support or their family, and write down some ideas of ways to help them prepare. List how you can best support the family and the individual. Discuss this with a colleague and keep the notes on file ready for use.

The role that advocacy can play in the support of people with autism

Let's first consider the role of self-advocacy and the value of supporting people with autistic spectrum conditions to speak up for themselves. For many individuals we support this is something that will need no teaching, only encouragement. It is something that will come very naturally and you are more likely to have trouble stopping them from speaking up about what is important to them. However, this will not always be the case. In *The Autistic Spectrum*, Dr Lorna Wing reminds us of the different personality types within the spectrum and although many people are able to speak for themselves, many cannot and some will passively receive whatever happens to them. It is almost as if they don't realise they can object or request something different.

We can teach some self advocacy skills and we can help with the understanding of the difference between being assertive and being rude. However, for those unable to speak, we need to look to others to advocate for them. This is very likely to be a parent or other significant family member or friend or advocacy support from an independent advocacy organisation. Advocacy organisations can provide somebody committed to getting alongside the person with autism and speaking on their behalf. They are there purely to get to know an individual, get to know their autism and then seek to advocate on their behalf.

The government strategy for England, *Fulfilling and Rewarding Lives*, says that autism awareness training is essential for any advocates looking to work with individuals with autistic spectrum conditions. There is a danger that if they are not autism aware then they will be guided by the values of choice and control, without realising how difficult these ideas are for people with autism. So many people with autism will choose what is familiar even if they don't like it, or seek control by restricting their lives even when they would like to move to new accommodation or experience a foreign holiday.

We have returned once more to the central importance of training and ensuring that people who work in the field of autistic spectrum conditions have a good level of knowledge of the nature of autism and how it impacts upon people in different ways. It is important to keep learning, and wherever possible, to learn from people who live with autistic spectrum conditions, as they are the real experts.

Thinking point

Can you think of a phrase that someone with autistic spectrum conditions has said that has really made you think? If so write it down and think about it. For me, just recently, it was John who said:

The hardest transition for me, Sue, happens each day when I have to get out of bed and step into the world that is so often confusing and at times quite terrifying.

Activity

Find out about the advocacy organisations in your area. Do they support people with autism and if so what kind of autism awareness training have their advocates received?

Key points from this chapter

- Workers often come and go in the lives of people with autism; families are there with them for much longer. This means people need to work together and listen to family members and take notice of their knowledge and experience.

- There are a range of interventions that claim to help people with autism learn and develop – it is important to find out about them in order to use the best methods to support the person well.

- Sensory overload can often occur when we are not thinking ahead. If we think ahead and plan well, problems can be prevented.

- Safeguarding training needs to be applied in an autism friendly way in order to really help people to stay safe.

- Making links to an advocacy organisation for someone you support can be very beneficial for them to get their voice heard.

References and where to go for more information

References

A is for Autism (DVD) (1992) London: BFI

Attfield, A and Morgan, H (2007) *Living with Autistic Spectrum Disorder.* London: Paul Chapman Publishing

Bickerton, S (2011) *Principles of Safeguarding and Protection for Learning Disability Workers.* Exeter: Learning Matters and BILD

Cohen, M J and Slone, D L (2008) *Visual Supports for People with Autism.* Bethesda, MD: Woodbine House Publishers

Gray, C (2000) *From Both Sides Now – How to Teach Social Understanding.* Paper presented at The Autism Europe Congress, Glasgow

Kaufman, B N (1994) *Son-Rise, the Miracle Continues.* Tiburon, CA: H J Kramer

Lovass, O I (1987) Behavioural treatment and normal educational and intellectual function in young children. *Journal of Consulting and Clinical Psychology*, Volume 55, pp. 3–9

Mezibov, G B (1997) Formal and informal measure of the effectiveness of the TEACCH programme. *Autism. International Journal of Research and Practice* 1, pp. 25–35

Tilly, L (2011) *Person Centred Approaches when Supporting People with a Learning Disability.* Exeter: Learning Matters and BILD

Wing, L (2003) *The Autistic Spectrum.* London: Robinson Publishers

Legislation, policies and reports

Department of Health (2001) *Valuing People – A New Strategy for Learning Disability for the 21st Century.* Norwich: TSO

Department of Health (2009) *Valuing People Now – The Government Strategy for People with Learning Disabilities.* Norwich: TSO

Department of Health (2010) *Fulfilling and Rewarding Lives – The Strategy for Adults with Autism in England.* Norwich: TSO

Websites

National Autistic Society Website www.autism.org.uk

Autism Education Trust Website www.autismeducationtrust.org.uk

Helen Sanderson Associates for information on person centred planning and approaches www.helensandersonassociates.co.uk

Glossary

Advocacy – getting someone to advocate for you or on your behalf, to speak up for you and ensure you get the right support.

Asperger syndrome – Asperger syndrome is a condition on the autism spectrum, named after Hans Asperger who described it in 1944, the year after Leo Kanner published his observations. People with Asperger syndrome will have average or higher level intelligence and develop speech and language normally. However, they will have the difficulties in communication and social interaction that are experienced by all people with autism and may also have sensory difficulties.

Autism spectrum condition (autistic spectrum conditions) – autism is a lifelong developmental disability. The word 'spectrum' is used because whilst all people with autism experience difficulties in the same areas (that is, they all have problems with communication, social interaction, ways of thinking and sensory processing), autism affects people in a wide variety of different ways. Those most severely impacted upon by their autistic spectrum conditions can be seen as at one end of the spectrum, whilst those who are able to function easily with little or no support can be seen as being at the other end of the spectrum.

Central coherence – this is the ability to see the larger picture as well as details when entering a room, looking at a picture, doing a task, etc. Many people with autistic spectrum conditions appear to struggle to see that bigger picture and will focus on a detail that may seem insignificant to others but is of major significance to them.

Classic autism – another name for Kanner's autism.

Communication – the way that two or more people make contact, build relationships and share messages. These messages can be ideas, thoughts or feelings as well as information and questions. Communication involves both sending and understanding these messages and can be done through many different ways including speech, writing, pictures, symbols, signs, pointing and body language, for example.

Echolalia – echolalia is the automatic repetition of words or phrases just spoken by another person. This can make somebody with autistic spectrum conditions appear to understand more than they really do.

Executive function – this is our ability to plan ahead and know what is needed. It is about the ability to shift attention from one thing to another when needed. It is also about our ability to decide not to do something because we realise the negative consequence. Many people with autistic spectrum conditions have poor executive functioning skills.

High functioning autism – high functioning autism is used to describe somebody who has autistic spectrum conditions, but does not have a learning disability. This term is sometimes used as if it had the same meaning as Asperger syndrome.

Intensive interaction – intensive interaction is an approach for teaching communication abilities to children and adults who have autism, severe learning difficulties, and profound and multiple learning difficulties who are still at early stages of development.

Kanner's autism – the term Kanner's autism is used in recognition of the observations published by Leo Kanner in 1943. He was the first person to formally document the condition we now call autism spectrum condition. Kanner identified all three of the triad of impairments as well as sensory processing difficulties.

Learning disability – a learning disability includes the presence of a significantly reduced ability to understand new or complex information and to learn new skills, together with a reduced ability to cope independently. A person's learning disability would start before adulthood, and it would have a lasting effect on their development.

Makaton – a system of supportive communication that uses signs with the spoken word to try and improve understanding and the ability to express oneself.

Neurology – neurology is the area of medicine concerned with the diagnosis, research and treatment of disorders of the nervous system, that is, the brain, the spinal cord and the nerves.

Neurotypical – neurotypical is a term used to describe people who are not on the autism spectrum. The neurological development of neurotypical people is consistent with what most people would perceive as normal, particularly with respect to their ability to process linguistic information and social cues.

Person centred planning – person centred planning is used to describe placing the individual and their needs at the centre of planning any support they require. For somebody with autistic spectrum conditions this means focusing on the person but also on how their autism impacts on their life.

Pervasive developmental disorder not otherwise specified (PDD-NOS) – used to describe when someone has severe and pervasive impairments in all three parts of the triad of impairments but does not have autism.

Picture Exchange Communication System (PECS) – a specific structured communication system used mainly in schools with children who have autism that teaches them what communication is for as well as how to communicate their wants and needs.

Processing delay – a processing delay is commonly experienced by people with autistic spectrum conditions. It means they may take much longer than most other people to understand and digest spoken or written information or to answer a question.

Proprioceptive sense – this is our sense of knowing where we are in space, for example how we are able to judge getting through a doorway when carrying a large object. Many people with autism have sensory issues including with their proprioceptive sense.

Self advocacy – to speak up for yourself, to advocate for yourself and ensure your own needs are met.

Sensory issues – sensory issues are experienced by almost all people on the autistic spectrum, who very often process their senses differently or have problems with one or more of their senses. People with autistic spectrum conditions may find they are overwhelmed by one or more of their senses or they may seek sensory stimulation that appears excessive. The usual five senses (hearing, seeing, taste, touch and smell), as well as vestibular and proprioceptive senses, need to be considered when supporting somebody with autistic spectrum conditions.

Social stories – these are stories that describes a situation, skill or concept in terms of relevant social cues and which help to give an understanding of other peoples' perspectives on a situation. They were designed by Carol Gray to help people with autism understand the workings of the social world better.

Special interests – most people with autistic spectrum conditions have subjects or objects that bring them particular pleasure and delight in life. They can be called obsessions but this is not really correct and the term special interest makes clearer the delight and pleasure that they bring to the life of the individual.

The triad of impairments – the triad of impairments describes three areas in which all people on the autism spectrum have difficulty: problems with communication, problems with social interaction and problems with ways of thinking and behaving.

Theory of mind – this is our ability to be in someone else's shoes, to empathise and be aware that people can think differently from us. People with autistic spectrum conditions have particular difficulties in this area.

Uneven cognitive profile – the uneven cognitive profile of people with autism means they have skills or talents in one area that are not consistent with their general level of ability. For example, somebody with autistic spectrum conditions and a learning disability, who cannot dress themselves or cross a road without help, may have a brilliant memory for dates and the specific details of past events. Very occasionally, the uneven cognitive profile includes an outstanding talent in one particular area, such as being able to draw to scale or play the piano to a very high standard.

Vestibular sense – our vestibular sense is our sense of balance.

Index

Added to a page number 'g' denotes glossary.